Psalm 15

Psalm 15

Integrating Faith and Work

DAVID WESLEY WHITLOCK
GORDON DUTILE
EDITORS

FOREWORD BY C. PAT TAYLOR

Featuring Contributions From:

Troy Bethards, Ronda O. Credille,
Timothy DeClue, Gordon Dutile,
Marinell Erven, Shelly Francka,
Susan Lynch, Rodger W. Minatra,
R. Stanton Norman, Rodney Reeves,
Tom D. Stevens, David W. Whitlock

RESOURCE *Publications* · Eugene, Oregon

PSALM 15
Integrating Faith and Work

ISBN 13: 978-1-49825-111-2

Manufactured in the U.S.A.

Contents

Acknowledgments

THIS DEVOTIONAL book is an abbreviated version of the book, *A Noble Calling: Devotions and Essays for Business Professionals*, published by Wipf and Stock Publishers, Resource Publications, Eugene, Oregon (see www.anoblecalling.com). *A Noble Calling* presents expanded essays on integrating a biblical worldview with business and professional life. Contributors to *A Noble Calling* hope that readers will be impressed to free themselves from the false dichotomy that pits ministry over and against the conduct of business and professional life—that readers will be liberated from a mindset that artificially separates the Christian life and spirituality from the professional life. The book is available from www.wipfandstock.com and other booksellers.

Psalm 15: Integrating Faith and Work is the result of collaboration by colleagues of Southwest Baptist University, who are dedicated to promoting the concept of applying a biblical worldview to one's profession. In addition to chapter contributors, the following individuals are acknowledged for their contributions, suggestions, and encouragement:

Rhonda Agee

Sharla Bailey

Wayne Clark

James Cain

Ashley Dinwiddie

Judy Dutile

Tina Campbell Owens

J. D. Lynch

Scarlettah Schaefer

C. Pat Taylor

Jenell Wagner

Carrie Wolcott

Dana Leigh Whitlock

Contributors

Troy Bethards is an Assistant Professor at Southwest Baptist University. He holds the BS from Southwest Baptist University, the MBA from Missouri State University, and the DBA from Anderson University.

Ronda O. Credille is an Associate Professor of Business Administration at Southwest Baptist University. She holds a BS from Southwest Baptist University, an MBA from Drury College, and the PhD from the University of Nebraska.

Timothy DeClue is Chair and Professor of Computer and Information Sciences at Southwest Baptist University. He holds the BS from Northwest Missouri State University and the MS and PhD from Southern Illinois University.

Gordon Dutile is the Provost at Southwest Baptist University where he also served for many years as a professor of Greek. He holds a B.S. from Louisiana Tech University, and the MDiv and PhD from Southwestern Baptist Theological Seminary. His previous book, *A Noble Calling: Devotions and Essays for business Professionals*, is available from Resource Publications at www.wipfandstock.com.

Marinell Rayfield Erven is a retired school administrator and currently serves as the Administrative Assistant for the College of Business and Computer Science at Southwest Baptist University. She holds the BS from Missouri State University, and the MS from Drury University.

Shelly Francka is the MBA Director at Southwest Baptist University. She holds her BS and MBA from Southwest Baptist University, and is a PhD student at Northwest University.

Susan Lynch is Chair and Professor of Business Administration at Southwest Baptist University. She holds a BA from Southwest Baptist University, the MSE from Central Missouri State University, and the EdD from the University of Arkansas.

Rodger W. Minatra is an Associate Professor of Business Administration at Southwest Baptist University. He holds a BS from Arizona State University, an MA from the University of Denver, and the EdD from the University of North Texas.

R. Stanton Norman serves as the Vice President for University Relations at Southwest Baptist University. He holds a BA from Criswell College, and the MDiv and PhD from Southwestern Baptist Theological Seminary.

Rodney Reeves serves as the Dean of The Courts Redford College of Theology and Ministry, and as Professor of Biblical Studies at Southwest Baptist University. He holds a BA from Southwest Baptist University, the MDiv and PhD from Southwestern Baptist Theological Seminary, and has completed additional study at Oxford University.

Tom D. Stevens is an Instructor of Economics at Southwest Baptist University. He holds a BS from Southwest Baptist University, a MTS from Dallas Theological Seminary, and an MBA from Southern Methodist University.

David W. Whitlock serves as the Associate Provost, Dean of the College of Business and Computer Science, and Professor of Business Administration at Southwest Baptist University. He holds the BS and MBA. from Southeastern Oklahoma State University, and the PhD from the University of Oklahoma. His previous books with Resource Publications include: *Opportunity: Introducing Free Enterprise and Business*, and A *Noble Calling: Devotions and Essays for Business Professionals*.

Foreword

C. Pat Taylor

IN *PSALM 15: Integrating Faith and Work*, Dr. Whitlock and Dr. Dutile have compiled a series of devotions by professionals who practice what they preach. The contributors to this small volume are Christians who daily live out their faith in their personal and professional lives. I know. I work with them daily.

Too often, Christians attempt to compartmentalize life and behave as if we live in a dichotomous world. This book of devotions challenges readers to develop the character traits of someone who may, as Psalm 15 says, "dwell with God." It is imperative in today's society that professionals develop a biblical worldview for all facets of life, including ministry and professional careers. Spirituality should not be divorced from professional life, and this project is an excellent reminder for professionals who desire to integrate faith and professional life. I know you will enjoy the insights and devotions in this book and encourage you to share it with others.

C. Pat Taylor
President
Southwest Baptist University

Introduction

A Psalm 15 Leader

David Wesley Whitlock

For years, students and professionals alike have expressed concern over their chosen field of study or choice of profession. For many, this struggle has often centered on a false dichotomy that lives on in spite of the efforts of the sixteenth century reformers who, among other critical issues of doctrine and ecclesiology, advanced the perspective of equality before God between the clergy and laity. Too often individuals, who have been called to practice their gifts and talents in the field of business and professional life, sense that to serve God they ought to be doing something more directly involved with the church. Many successful business leaders, upon coming to faith in Christ or upon renewing their interest in God's Word, struggle with whether or not they should enter vocational ministry. Certainly, God calls some from among the professions into such vocations, but I am convinced that many simply haven't realized the full potential of where God has placed them.

One of my mentors in higher education is Dr. Bob Agee. Dr. Agee, years ago, seemed to sense that I was struggling with this very issue, even though I had not revealed my thoughts to him. He looked at me intently and spoke about the stewardship of experience. He explained that God desires to use everything I have experienced including my education and work life. Everything. While I suppose that reality should have been self-evident, Dr. Agee's advice was like a thunderbolt. God desires to use *everything*. There is great freedom in realizing that the calling to business and professional life is every bit as valid and significant to Kingdom work as the calling to vocational ministry.

In the years since then, I have become increasingly convinced of this truth and of the fact that God's people who are assigned duties in corporate board rooms, offices, on sales forces, in entrepreneurial ventures, and as members of research and development teams, are among his most effective servants. Individuals who are active in the marketplace are among his most treasured ministers and have the potential to have a wider impact and larger influence than many full-time pastors and ministers. Likewise, these professionals have a capacity for great harm to the church and the cause of Christ, if while making claims of belief their actions prove inconsistent with what God's Word teaches—if their walk doesn't match their talk.

I am convinced that what Dr. Agee instilled in me so many years ago is true. God wants to use you, right now, where you are, and he desires to sanctify all of your experiences for His purposes. What God desires for his followers is that they walk uprightly, speak truth, deal fairly, honor him, keep their word, and reach out to others—that they love the Lord with all their heart, mind, strength, and love others as themselves. Psalm 15 summarizes this kind of person as it describes a person *who dwells with God,* and its words ought to characterize the follower of God who represents him in the conduct of business.

Psalm 15

The Character of Those Who May Dwell with the LORD
LORD, who may abide in Your tabernacle?
Who may dwell in Your holy hill?
He who walks uprightly,
And works righteousness,
And speaks the truth in his heart;
He who does not backbite with his tongue,
Nor does evil to his neighbor,
Nor does he take up a reproach against his friend;
In whose eyes a vile person is despised,
But he honors those who fear the LORD;
He who swears to his own hurt and does not change;
He who does not put out his money at usury,
Nor does he take a bribe against the innocent.
He who does these things shall never be moved (NKJV).

It is not an exaggeration to say that such a person is not only a good ambassador for Christ but also that such a person is pleasing to God. For those called into vocations involving entrepreneurial ventures, professional careers, and positions in business—take heed. Your calling is noble. Determine to honor God in all your dealings. Dedicate yourself to being a *Psalm 15 professional*—a *Psalm 15 leader*.

At SBU, faculty in the College of Business and Computer Science intentionally integrate their disciplines with a biblical worldview. Through the College's Psalm 15 Faith Integration Plan, faculty adopted eight characteristics inspired by the fifteenth Psalm that should epitomize the character of each graduate. These characteristics include: Integrity, Service, Respect, Charity, Faithfulness, Truthfulness, Humility, and Perseverance.

DWW

I

Integrity

The Essence of Integrity

Gordon Dutile

The Hebrew concept translated by the English word *integrity* communicates the ideas of completeness, soundness, wholeness, and purity. Even after Job had lost his family and all of his possessions, God said to Satan, "Have you considered My servant Job? For there is no one like him on the earth, a blameless and upright man fearing God and turning away from evil. And he still holds fast his integrity, although you incited Me against him, to ruin him without cause" (Job 2:3 NASB). It is the overarching essence of character. A person of integrity reflects the qualities of life that commend themselves to others. Integrity demonstrates strength of character that enables the individual, regardless of circumstances, to live out what Romans teaches. "And we know that God causes all things to work together for good to those who love God, to those who are called according to His purpose" (Rom. 8:28 NASB).

Consider Joseph who as a young man, probably a teenager, was sold by his jealous brothers into slavery. Many would have used his terrible circumstances as an excuse to give up and have a pity party. Instead Joseph revealed a rock-solid confidence in the sovereign God of Israel to guide, protect, and provide for him. He found himself in an Egyptian home and exhibited such responsibility that he ended up as the manager of the household. When he resisted the sexual advances of his master's wife, she falsely accused him of attempted rape. He wound up in prison during which time he befriended the baker and cupbearer of the Egyptian Pharaoh, helping each of them interpret his dream. His only request of them was that when they got out, they would not forget him; however, he was forgotten. Ultimately, Joseph was remembered and became second in command in Egypt. He not only helped to save the Egyptian people during a difficult famine, but he became the instrument in the deliverance of his father's family including his brothers who had sold him into slavery. His actions and responses during this saga were a demonstration of unquestionable integrity. He opted to exhibit self-control when he had the opportunity to fulfill self-gratification. He revealed trust in God when he could have yielded to despair and self-pity. He exercised forgiveness and compassion when he could have reacted in a spirit of anger and vengeance.

Proverbs has the following to say about the person of integrity. "He stores up sound wisdom for the upright; He is a shield to those who walk in integrity" (Prov. 2:7 NASB). "He who walks in integrity walks securely, but he who perverts his ways will be found out" (Prov. 10:9 NASB). "The integrity of the upright will guide them, but the crookedness of the treacherous will destroy them" (Prov. 11:3 NASB). "A righteous man who walks in integrity—how blessed are his sons after him" (Prov. 20:7 NASB). "Better is the poor who walks in integrity than he who is crooked though he be rich" (Prov. 28:6 NASB).

The Greek word used in the New Testament that I think most closely communicates *integrity* is a word that is often translated as *pure* or *sincere*. The root idea of the word is *unalloyed*. This Greek word is a combination of the words *sun* and *to judge*. It was used at times to describe the picture of a buyer examining a piece of glassware in the sunlight to determine if the merchant was attempting to cover a crack in the item by filling it with wax.

A Christian life characterized by integrity is able to withstand the scrutiny of a skeptical world. When placed under such intense examination, it reveals itself as unmixed, unalloyed, pure and sincere. This quality is exhibited in the life of one who has a personal relationship with the Lord Jesus. That relationship is constantly growing and is empowered by the Holy Spirit. The person of integrity is quick to realize that pride goes before a fall and, therefore, humbly recognizes her or his total dependence on the grace and mercy of God.

It is important to focus on the concept of unmixed, unalloyed, and pure. It is not an accident or coincidence that the first commandment is, "You shall have no other gods before Me" (Exod. 20:3 NASB). In response to the question as to which commandment is the most important, Jesus said it this way: "The foremost is, 'Hear, O Israel; the Lord our God is one Lord; and you shall love the Lord your God with all your heart, and with all your soul, and with all your mind, and with all your strength'" (Mark 12:29–30 NASB). To be a person of biblical integrity, he or she must be single-minded. There cannot be any split allegiance. In teaching the Bible, I have often noted that the appropriate approach to the Christian life is to be sold out to God. If our allegiance and commitment are to God and God alone, all other aspects or areas of life will be managed and cared for appropriately. If Jesus is Lord of all, He will guide the believer to do the right thing in every relationship and situation. We will not have to make a list of who or what comes next. The Lord will lead us to do what is right and best. Paul's prayer for the Philippians was, "And this I pray, that your love may abound still more and more in real knowledge and all discernment, so that you may approve the things that are excellent, in order to be sincere and blameless until the day of Christ" (Phil. 1:9–10 NASB). The Christian whose life is characterized by integrity is able to distinguish not only that which is good but that which is most excellent, that which is best.

I shall never forget the example set for me by a dear saint who was a member of the church that I served as associate pastor while I was in seminary. She worked for the government in a clerical area. She told me that when she was at her job, she did not take time away from her responsibilities to witness or to read her Bible. Her commitment to God and His rule in her life led her to believe that she was to be the best employee possible. To use *company time* to witness when she was being paid to work was an act of dishonesty and would be hurtful to her testimony as a Christian. When she was on her allowed breaks during the day, she actively looked for the opportunity to share her faith. Her focus in life was to be what God wanted her to be. She was single-minded in her purpose, unmixed in her motives. That enabled her to see all of life as a means to serve God. That commitment made her a better church member, wife, mother, friend, and employee. She exemplified to me what Paul meant when the Spirit led him to write, "Whether, then, you eat or drink or whatever you do, do all to the glory of God" (1 Cor. 10:31 NASB).

In summary, Christian integrity does not mean that the individual has reached a state of flawless perfection. It is, however, a virtue that results from the believer maturing in the image of Christ and growing more and more aware of her or his absolute dependence on the power provided by God. The textbook for integrity is the Word of God. Timothy received the following admonition from his mentor: "Be diligent to present yourself approved to God as a workman who does not need to be ashamed, handling accurately the word of truth" (1 Tim. 2:15 NASB). The Christian who exhibits this quality will always exclaim along with the apostle Paul, "But by the grace of God I am what I am, and His grace toward me did not prove vain." (1 Cor. 15:10a NASB).

An Ethics Primer

Troy Bethards

Insider Trading. Falsified audits. Inordinately high CEO salaries. Mismanagement of pension funds. From Enron and WorldCom to the local clothing store owner who secretly videotapes clients in the dressing room, business is often portrayed as corrupt and manipulated by dishonest and immoral individuals. Though there are many professionals who perform their responsibilities ethically and legally, the headlines reveal the sad truth that many in business are driven by baser instincts. When faced with ethical dilemmas, how should the believer respond? The following ethical frameworks should be understood by all professionals and those preparing for careers in business.

Theological Framework: The theological framework is important for Christians because believers recognize that they answer to a higher authority and seek God's guidance and direction in their lives. Making sure that their actions align with God's desire greatly influences their decision making. Therefore, the primary question in ethical decision making is, "What is the desire of God?" To properly address this question, the theological system places its focus on the love for God and mankind, as well as respect for others.

Addressing the importance of love as a basis for determining morality, Hill references "ethicist Lewis Smedes [who] characterizes love as 'the hinge for every other moral rule to swing on.'"[1] The source for using the love for God and mankind is found in Matthew: "Jesus replied: 'Love the Lord your God with all of your heart and with all of your soul and with all your mind.' This is the first and greatest

---

1. Hill, A. (1997). *Just Business: Christian Ethics for the Marketplace.* Downers Grove, IL: Intervarsity Press, p. 47.

commandment. And the second is like it: 'Love your neighbor as yourself'" (Matt. 25:37–39 NIV).

Another aspect of the theological framework is respect. Respect for all mankind is reinforced in 1 Peter: "Show proper respect for everyone: Love the brotherhood of believers, fear God, honor the king" (1 Pet. 2:17 NIV). If this framework were used to come to an appropriate conclusion, one must answer the question of whether a specific business action interferes or misdirects a person's love for God and His ways. One must also consider whether a particular action encroaches upon the command to love and respect others. If the action violates any of these positions, then it should be considered unethical. For Christians, the theological framework would be an important component in concluding whether a particular situation or action is acceptable.

Legal Framework: Carl Fulda indicates how legal requirements can be used as an ethical framework when he states, "The law reflects the thought prevailing in the community, including its moral values, and thus it becomes a basis of business ethics."[2] Therefore, it could be said that if enough people within a democratic society deemed a particular action unethical, then that society would establish laws preventing such action. This statement would indicate that everyone has an equal voice in the determination of such laws; however, that is usually not the case.[3] Special interest groups influence legal considerations, which may not be the desire of the majority in a society. Hosmer also points out that even advocates of the legal framework will indicate that this system establishes only minimal standards as moral judgments.[4] It seems evident that the legal framework has shortcomings. Even so, the rules of law may still be used as a guide in determining whether a particular action is appropriate and provide an indication of how a society feels about a particular action.

Economic Framework: One of the components of capitalism, as set forth by Adam Smith, is the ability of individuals to better

2. Stevens, E. (1979). *Business Ethics*. New York, NY. Paulist Press, p. 118.

3. Hosmer, L. T. (1996). *The Ethics of Management* (Third Ed.). Irwin/McGraw-Hill, p. 74.

4. Ibid, p. 62.

themselves. Individuals are rewarded under a capitalist system when they are better suited for certain positions, have special talents or have special information. One aspect of the capitalist system is captured by Shaw and Barry when they state the following ideal that coincides with Adam Smith's *Invisible Hand* doctrine: "We will, if left free, engage in labor and exchange goods in a way that results in the greatest benefit to society."[5]

Utilitarianism Framework: Utilitarianism is focused on the outcome. The goal is to pursue the greatest positive result for the greatest number of people. The utilitarianism framework can be viewed from two different perspectives. Jeremy Bentham and John Stuart Mill are credited with developing utilitarianism or more specifically *act utilitarianism*. Act utilitarianism specifies "that we must ask ourselves what the consequences of a particular act in a particular situation will be for all of those affected."[6] If the action in a particular situation will bring greater benefit compared to another alternative, it should be pursued; if not, then this action is not acceptable.

A second utilitarian perspective is *rule utilitarianism*, which is offered by Richard Brandt. This version states that moral codes should be used to apply the standard of utilitarianism rather than individual actions.[7] The focus should be on the moral codes that are most appropriate for society, so that satisfaction or utility is increased. Thus, rule utilitarianism is used to help determine whether an action is appropriate in general and not just as it pertains to a particular situation.

Justice Framework: Justice is an important value in America's society and is one of the values on which this nation was founded, as represented by the last portion of the *Pledge of Allegiance* of the United States, which concludes "with liberty and justice for all." As Hosmer addresses John Rawls' theory of *Distributive Justice*, he states that "Justice is felt to be the first virtue of social institutions, as truth

5. Shaw, W. H. and Barry, V. (1992). *Moral Issues on Business* (Fifth Ed). Belmont, CA Wadsworth, Inc., p. 157.

6. Ibid, p. 62.

7. Ibid, p. 78.

is the first virtue of systems of thought."[8] As a cornerstone in society, justice is utilized as a means to address ethical dilemmas.

There are three possible approaches to utilizing justice in an ethical dilemma. The first type of justice is *Compensatory Justice*, which attempts to appropriately compensate an individual who has been *wronged* in some manner. The second classification is *Retributive Justice*, which attempts to appropriate consequences to individuals who have engaged in an undesirable action. The final form of justice is *Distributive Justice*, which focuses on whether benefits and costs to society are distributed in a right, just or fair manner.

In Rawls' theory of Distributive Justice, cooperation of individuals is necessary for the promotion of society as a whole. The distribution of items that are of benefit can be handled in a number of ways. Benefits could be given in equal portion to each individual, according to a person's level of competence, according to what a person needs, how much an individual contributes or how much effort one expends.[9] Hosmer also points out that individuals will pursue a proper distribution of the benefits that society creates; and that this distribution of benefits will likely be unequal as long as it shows that the unequal system works to the benefit of everyone within a society.[10] Therefore, if it is determined, for example, that the distribution that results from insider trading is not just, or that cooperation between individuals is decreased, then the action is not acceptable. However, if trading with privileged information results in an appropriate distribution and increases cooperation between individuals, the action is ethical.

Many struggle with their call to a professional vocation. Business is often presented in unflattering light, especially as corporate scandals are plastered on newspaper headlines, the evening news, and nationally distributed magazines. But for the Christian, business can be a high and holy calling. Christian business professionals ought to approach their calling as sacred. When approached from the standpoint

---

8. Hosmer, L. T. (1996). *The Ethics of Management* (Third Ed.). Irwin/ McGraw-Hill., p. 95.

9. Ibid. p. 96.

10. Ibid.

that business is about meeting the needs of others, one's career goals can take on a whole new perspective.

Business and free enterprise are compatible with biblical practices and expectations if approached with the view of providing housing, clothing, food, and products that improve the lives of its users. Innovation that improves the health, welfare, and provides needed goods and services for others, when done ethically and in accordance with biblical principles and expectations, is a noble calling. When approached from the standpoint of serving others, the practice of business becomes a worthy profession to pursue. Servant leadership and meeting the needs of others is indeed a calling that is consistent with a Christian worldview, if it is practiced according to the high standards set forth in God's Word.

2

Service

Putting Others First

Ronda O. Credille

THE SNOWFLAKES were so large that I used an umbrella as I carefully walked through the parking lot to my office building early one morning. Though the snow had been falling for little more than an hour, the parking lot was already covered with a thick blanket of white. *The physical plant crew probably hasn't had time to shovel the sidewalk either,* I thought to myself. The sidewalk slopes downward from the parking lot to the building and becomes slippery during winter precipitation. But to my surprise and relief, the sidewalk was clear.

Later in the day, I learned that the housekeeper for the building, Chong "Lena" Campbell, a petite native of Korea, had shoveled the sidewalk before she began her regularly assigned duties indoors; a fellow faculty member had spotted her in action. She knew the physical plant crew would not be able to get to our sidewalk before college students and faculty members arrived for early morning classes. So she took the task upon herself. Lena rendered a tremendous service to a hundred or so members of the university family, yet if she had not been caught in the act, no one would have known that she was our benefactor.

What is Service? The word *service* is a familiar term in the American vocabulary. Approximately 80% of the U.S. economy is service-based.[1] Occupations in the service sector, specifically in the

1. *Service Sector Extends Advance but Signals Pace Might Slow* (2007,

health and computer programming industries, are forecasted to provide most of the new jobs created in the near future.[2] Businesses often tout their customer service in advertisements. Not coincidentally, a survey conducted by the Mystery Shopping Providers Association indicated that 93% of the 3,500 people surveyed considered "employee courtesy and employee knowledge" to be "the most important elements" of a shopping experience.[3]

With so much emphasis on service, it would seem logical to have people lining up for positions as servants. Yet it is rare to hear the latter mentioned outside of religious circles. What image comes to mind when you think of the word servant? A French maid? A British butler? Servant often connotes someone who performs household tasks, perhaps of a menial nature.

One of the greatest leaders of the New Testament church was the apostle Paul, yet he referred to himself as, "Paul, a servant of God" (Titus 1:1 NIV), and "Paul, a servant of Christ Jesus" (Rom. 1:1 NIV). One might wonder if his humility stemmed from the fact that his actions had led to the martyrdom of many Christians. That explanation is unlikely. Paul instructed believers to, "*Serve* one another in love" (Gal. 5:13 NIV italics added) and to serve employers (literally, masters) "wholeheartedly, as if you were serving the Lord" (Eph. 6:7 NIV).

Charles Swindoll states that God's main objective for His children is to build into them "the same serving and giving qualities" that "made Jesus distinct from all others in His day."[4] Swindoll acknowledges that this is "a lifestyle totally at variance with the world system."[5] Human nature is concerned with not only self-preservation, but self-

---

February 6). The Wall Street Journal, A2. Retrieved March 24, 2007 from http://online.wsj.com/public.

2. *Futurist; Jan/Feb2007 Supplement, Vol. 41*, p. 7. High-Paying Careers of the Next Two Decades. http://search.ebscohost.com. Business Source Premier. March 24, 2007.

3. *No Mystery Here: Courtesy Counts.* (2006). Convenience Store News, 42(4), p. 8.

4. Swindoll, C. R. (1981). Improving Your Serve: The Art of Unselfish Living. Waco, Texas: Word, Inc., p. 18.

5. Ibid. p. 98.

advancement. No wonder some of the people of Thessalonica accused Paul and Silas of "upset[ting] the world" with their teachings" (Acts 17:6 NIV). John Beckett notes that the early disciples were modeling Christ because they "understood the joy of sacrifice and the reward in serving."[6] Following the example of their Lord, they "extend[ed] themselves on the behalf of others."[7] His phrase encapsulates the idea of servanthood.

The late Bob Briner, former president of ProServ Television, observed, "The conventional wisdom [in business] is that to be number one, you must take care of number one."[8] Briner contradicted this assumption by referring to Jesus' declaration in *Matthew* 23:11: "The greatest among you will be your servant." Briner explained, "This kind of servanthood require[s] an attitude that asks, "How can I best take care of the needs of my employees and customers in the context of a growing, thriving business?"[9]

What Are the Characteristics of a Servant? Swindoll calls the Beatitudes (Matt. 5:1–12) "the most descriptive word-portrait of a servant ever recorded."[10] Swindoll goes on to say that Jesus "has described our calling by explaining our role as:

> Poor in spirit
> Mourning
> Gentle
> Hungering and thirsting for righteousness
> Merciful
> Pure in heart
> Peacemakers
> Persecuted[11]

6. Beckett, J. D. (1998). Loving Monday. Downers Grove, Illinois: InterVarsity Press, p. 117.

7. Ibid. p. 117.

8. Briner, B. (1996). *The Management Methods of Jesus: Ancient Wisdom for Modern Business.* Nashville, Tennessee: Thomas Nelson, Inc., p. 57.

9. Ibid. p. 58.

10. Swindoll, C. R. (1981). *Improving Your Serve: The Art of Unselfish Living.* Waco, Texas: Word, Inc., p. 98.

11. Ibid.

Beckett identifies two prerequisites to genuine servanthood: sincere motivations and a biblical foundation.[12] The Apostle Paul warned Timothy about people "who think that godliness is a means to financial gain" (1 Tim. 6:5 NIV). Those who serve for the purpose of being noticed or repaid are not true servants; they merely view acts of service as a means of personal gain. Dr. John Wheeler, a college professor and a preaching elder at Wellspring Fellowship in Bolivar, Missouri, reminds our congregation regularly that we are to minister to people at the point of their need—not at the point of our need to minister. Paul declared that, "we are God's workmanship, created in Christ Jesus to do good works, which God prepared in advance for us to do" (Eph. 2:10 NIV). Biblical service means performing the works that "God prepared in advance for us to do," not *hustling* (Dr. Wheeler is also a former collegiate football coach) to find something to do so we can meet our daily service quota.

Born (Again) to Serve. King David acknowledged, "All the days ordained for me were written in your book before one of them came to be" (Ps. 139:16 NIV). When Mordecai urged Esther to plead with King Xerxes for mercy on the Jewish people, Mordecai said, "And who knows but that you have come to royal position for such a time as this?" (Est. 4:14 NIV). The ultimate servant, Jesus, said of Himself, "For even the Son of Man did not come to be served, but to serve, and to give His life as a ransom for many" (Mark 10:45 NIV). If God's desire is for those who have been born again (John 3:3 NIV) to imitate His Son, then all believers are to be servants. Simon Peter's mother-in-law was quite literally saved to serve. In Luke we read that she was "suffering from a high fever" (Luke 4:38–39 NIV). Jesus healed her and "she got up at once and began to wait" on Him and everyone who had gathered in Simon Peter's home. The Apostle Paul declares in Galatians that God, "set [him] apart from birth and called [him] by grace" (Gal. 1:15 NIV) to serve the Gentiles by preaching the Gospel to them.

Prepared to Serve. The forty days Jesus spent in the desert being tempted by Satan were a means of preparation for both His ministry and crucifixion. The Gospels tell us that "Jesus often withdrew to

12. Beckett, J. D. (1998). *Loving Monday.* Downers Grove, Illinois: InterVarsity Press, p. 120.

lonely places and prayed" (Luke 5:16; Mark 1:35 NIV). After his Damascus road experience, Paul spent three years in Arabia preparing for his ministry to the Gentiles (Gal. 1:17–18 NIV). Prayer and meditation in the Word are two ways to prepare for service.

Humbled to Serve. The subtitle of Swindoll's book *Improving Your Serve* is *The Art of Unselfish Living.* Can you think of anyone you know who is both proud and unselfish? The two traits are incompatible. Jesus told his followers, "If anyone would come after me, he must deny himself and take up his cross daily and follow me" (Luke 9:23 NIV). Paul instructs us in Romans, "Do not think of yourself more highly than you ought . . . Honor one another above yourselves . . . Do not be proud" (Rom. 12:3, 9, 16 NIV). The Gospels provide examples of Peter exhibiting the very human trait of pride (e.g., "Even if all fall away on account of you, I never will" Matt. 26:33 NIV). Jesus knew that Peter needed to be humbled in order to become a bold servant following the resurrection, thus he told Peter, "[B]efore the rooster crows, you will disown me three times" (Matt. 26:34 NIV). Jesus did not leave Peter in his dejected state, however. Jesus restored Peter to fellowship as recorded in John 21:15–17. These events exemplify the statement Jesus made to His host, a prominent Pharisee, "Everyone who exalts himself will be humbled, and he who humbles himself will be exalted" (Luke 14:11 NIV).

What Are the Consequences and Rewards of Servanthood? Swindoll lists four potential consequences of servanthood identified by the Apostle Paul in 2 Cor. 4:8–9: affliction, confusion, persecution and rejection.[13] How are we to respond in these circumstances? According to James, we are to "consider it pure joy" (James 1:2 NIV). Once again, being a servant means behavior that is atypical by the world's standards. Is such a response possible for humans? When the Sanhedrin ordered Peter and the other apostles to be flogged for preaching the Gospel, they "rejoic[ed] because they had been counted worthy of suffering disgrace for the Name" (Acts 5:41 NIV).

Many companies offer rewards to loyal customers for their patronage. Airlines offer frequent-flyer miles, credit card companies

---

13. Swindoll, C. R. (1981). *Improving Your Serve: The Art of Unselfish Living.* Waco, Texas: Word, Inc., p. 178.

offer premiums, and some fast-food restaurants offer free food to customers who fill up their punch-cards. The rewards program for the servants of Jesus Christ, however, makes all others pale by comparison! The rewards that await His servants include all of the following:

> *A mansion*: "In my Father's house are many mansions: if it were not so, I would have told you. I go to prepare a place for you" (John 14.1–3 KJV).

> *A full life*: "I have come that they may have life, and have it to the full" ((John 10.9–11 NIV).

> *Eternal life*: "I give them eternal life, and they shall never perish; no one can snatch them out of my hand" (John 10:27–29 NIV).

> *More than we give up*: "'I tell you the truth,' Jesus replied, 'no one who has left home or brothers or sisters or mother or father or children or fields for me and the gospel will fail to receive a hundred times as much in this present age (homes, brothers, sisters, mothers, children and fields—and with them, persecutions) and in the age to come, eternal life'" (Mark 10:28–30 NIV).

> *All of our needs met*: "And my God will meet all your needs according to his glorious riches in Christ Jesus" (Phil. 4:19 NIV).

> *A crown*: "Now there is in store for me the crown of righteousness, which the Lord, the righteous Judge, will award to me on that day—and not only to me, but also to all who have longed for his appearing" (2 Tim. 4:8 NIV).

> *An inheritance*: "Now if we are children, then we are heirs—heirs of God and co-heirs with Christ, if indeed we share in his sufferings in order that we may also share in his glory" (Rom. 8:17 NIV).

And this list is not exhaustive. Paul, the self-described "servant of Christ Jesus" (Rom. 1:1 NIV) wrote, "I consider that our present sufferings are not worth comparing with the glory that will be revealed in us" (Rom. 8:18 NIV). Not too bad of a rewards program for a servant!

Free to Serve

Tom D. Stevens

The Dead Sea, located between Jordan and Israel, is the lowest surface point on earth at 1,371 feet below sea level. It also happens to be one of the saltiest bodies of water with salt concentrations nearly eight times greater than the ocean. Although the density of the Dead Sea's saltwater provides a good flotation surface for fascinated tourists, the heavy concentrations of salt make it nearly impossible for aquatic life to survive. Yet, despite the absence of life in the Dead Sea, over 150 sources of fresh water and aquatic life feed into the sea. How is it then that a body of water with so many sources of life cannot sustain life? The answer is simple. The Dead Sea has no outlets. When the fresh water and aquatic life enter the Dead Sea, the water becomes stagnant, salt forms, and the aquatic life dies.

I am convinced that we as Christians often suffer from the *Dead Sea effect* in our lives because we lack a critical outlet for our faith—service. Immersed within a consumption-driven society, we are deceived into believing that the freedom Jesus Christ has granted us is purely for our own good and enjoyment. Have you ever considered the possibility that we have been freed from the law of sin so that we might serve one another? This is the very message with which the Apostle Paul encouraged the Galatians, writing, "For you were called to freedom, brethren; only do not turn your freedom into an opportunity for the flesh, but through love serve one another" (Gal. 5:13 NASB). Are you using your freedom to serve?

As you seek to answer this question, it is helpful to reflect on the example of service displayed by our Lord and Savior, Jesus Christ. In Philippians, Paul writes of Christ and his human incarnation that he "made himself nothing, taking the very nature of a servant, being made in human likeness" (Phil. 2:7 NIV). What an incredible statement. What an incredible act by our Savior! Most of us spend our entire lives trying to become something or somebody. We seek to gain status, authority or wealth in hopes of building a lasting legacy. Yet, Christ, having all of the privileges of His Father, in an instant chose to lay aside his heavenly privileges and become nothing so that you and I might have everything. I suppose we could assert that Christ's act of humility sets a standard for service far beyond what we are capable of achieving. However, that would require us to ignore Paul's introductory words to this passage in which he urges, "Your attitude *should be the same* as that of Christ Jesus" (Phil. 2:5 NIV italics added).

By no means is it easy to lay aside our privileges for the sake of others. During my studies at seminary, I worked as a membership services coordinator at a YMCA located in a relatively affluent neighborhood. The very nature of my job was to serve the YMCA members, even on their less cordial days. I realized very soon that for most people my education, international experiences, and other résumé builders I identified myself with did not really matter. To most members, I was simply the guy who was responsible if there were not enough towels in the workout room; or, the guy to blame if the televisions were set to the wrong channel; or worse yet, the guy to call when the toilet was plugged in the bathroom. I recall thinking once as toilet water squirted onto my slacks from beneath the plunger, "this must be what the word *services* in *membership services* truly means." I eventually discovered a variety of reasons the word service was in my job title, many more of them equally unpleasant.

Although you may not be in a service profession, and your job title may not include the word *services*, as Christians we have all been called into the business of service. And despite what we might think from time to time, not a single one of us is overqualified for the job. In fact, the job has very little to do with qualifications and everything to do with attitude. In his letter to the Romans, Paul sought to remind the Christian community of this principle, writing, "Do not conform any longer to the pattern of this world, but be transformed by the renewing of your mind. Then you will be able to test and approve what God's will is—His good, pleasing and perfect will. For by the grace given me I say to every one of you: Do not think of yourself more highly than you ought, but rather think of yourself with sober judgment, in accordance with the measure of faith God has given you" (Rom. 12:2–3 NIV).

Thinking too highly of one's self was a problem common even among Jesus' disciples. On one occasion, after watching and hearing his disciples argue about position and power, Christ responded saying, "Not so with you. Instead, whoever wants to become great among you must be your servant, and whoever wants to be first must be your slave—just as the Son of Man did not come to be served, but to serve, and to give his life as a ransom for many" (Matt. 20:26–28 NIV). I love the first four words of these verses, "Not so with you." This could be the tagline for most of Jesus' teachings. The disciples, confronted by the same basic worldly influences we face today, were constantly comparing themselves to those around them. Yet, Jesus was continually reminding them that the principles of the Kingdom of God are in stark contrast to the principles of this world. The disciples were seeking greatness by being first, yet Jesus challenged them to seek greatness by being last.

Jesus' response to his disciples regarding power and position was not a declaration about what types of positions we should hold. In fact, some of the most sincere and servant-minded Christians I know hold rather prominent positions in their organizations. By no means is Jesus encouraging us to seek demotions in order to be real servants. If that were Jesus' message, it would be quite easy to achieve. Instead, Jesus' teaching is a statement about what our attitudes about ourselves and those around us should be regardless of the position we hold. As Jesus watched and heard his disciples argue over who would be the greatest among them, he recognized that their inward-focus was a paralyzing force that would prevent them from serving. Many of us today suffer from this same paralyzing force. Our inward-focus prevents us from living in the freedom we have been granted for the purpose of serving one another. So, how are you using your freedom?

In our quest to share Christ's servant attitude, it is important to recognize that the desire and ability to serve one another is not the natural crying of our hearts. This is a *no-brainer* for most of us. Perhaps this is why Paul wrote to the Galatians, "Through *love*, serve one another" (Gal. 5:13 NIV). But where does this love come from? Are we expected to magically conjure up this love so that we might then be motivated to serve? According to Paul, the love that enables us to serve is a fruit of the Spirit's work in our lives. As Paul asserted, "But the fruit of the Spirit is love, joy, peace, patience, kindness, goodness, faithfulness, gentleness, self-control; against such things there is no law" (Gal. 5:22–23 NIV). Not only has Christ freed us to serve one another, but he has also equipped us with the love, patience, kindness, goodness, and gentleness needed to truly serve one another. Yet, even though we are freed to serve and equipped to serve, the choice to serve is still a choice each one of us must make.

Perhaps the most spiritually dry period in my life was during seminary. I entered seminary, somewhat naively, with a variety of utopian expectations of what the experience would entail. Equipped with a passion to study and understand God's Word, I couldn't imagine a better place to spend two years of my life. Yet, within a few months, I found myself in a spiritual desert. Despite being fed weekly by some of the greatest biblical scholars and teachers in North America, I was unimpressed. So, I did what most of us do during such times. I devoted myself to my job, and I simply went through the motions of what was expected of me spiritually. How could this happen in such a spiritually rich environment?

At least part of the answer is found is Proverbs, which says, "He who is full loathes honey, but to the hungry even what is bitter tastes sweet" (Prov. 27:7 NIV). After only one semester of seminary, I was filled to the brim with sound Biblical teaching, to the point of loathing even the best sermon or devotion. However, the problem was not in my excessive consumption of such great teaching, but rather in my failure to use my training in service to others. Much like the Dead Sea, I had countless sources of life flowing into me; yet, failing to recognize the importance of service in my life, I had no outlets for my faith. Spiritually, I was stagnating and slowly dying inside. I was using the freedom granted me by Christ to serve myself rather than others. Yet, as I began to seek out opportunities at work, church, and throughout the community to serve, I once again began to experience the life that accompanies the freedom we have in Christ.

As the Apostle Paul wrote, "For you were called to freedom, brethren; only do not turn your freedom into an opportunity for the flesh, but through love serve one another" (Gal. 5:13 NASB). So, how are you using your freedom?

3

Respect

All I'm Asking For

Susan Lynch

Respect. Such a simple word. Unfortunately, the word is becoming somewhat outdated in our society. Many just don't take it as seriously as they should. Aretha Franklin asked for—actually demanded—respect. But it was all she really did insist upon. Comedian Rodney Dangerfield complained that it was the one thing he couldn't get. His whole act was built upon his tagline, "I don't get no respect." Both Franklin and Dangerfield longed for respect, but they are not alone. Yet, in many ways, it seems that our society has taken a step backward in regard to showing respect for others.

On a practical level, respect includes taking someone's feelings, needs, thoughts, ideas, wishes, and preferences into consideration. Giving someone respect demonstrates that we value the person as well as his thoughts and feelings. If we truly respect someone, we acknowledge him, listen to him, and are truthful with him. Respect also allows us to accept a person's individuality and idiosyncrasies.

I am convinced that every human deserves respect, from those in positions of authority to the least powerful among us—especially the least powerful. Respect is demonstrated through our behavior toward another person; respect is also felt by the recipient. Many of us act in ways that are considered respectful, and we also seem to have the ability to feel respect for someone. We seem to perceive when we are respected by someone else.

As a college professor, I have had the privilege to teach students from all over the world. I especially enjoy having in my classes students from our own nation's South. Their southern customs and manners are refreshing; they answer with "Yes, ma'am," or "Yes, sir." They seem inclined toward respectful behavior, at least in the classroom. But this respect isn't limited to a region. I grew up as a Northerner—a Wisconsinite—and I was taught the practice of respect in responding to my elders, too. But for some reason the practice just seems to be in short supply today.

Respect is a boomerang. You must send it out before it comes back to you. Respect cannot be demanded or forced. Respecting those in authority may seem like common sense, but many never learned that lesson. I grew up with the philosophy that a person must earn your respect; it's not something that is freely given. This philosophy made sense to me and it seemed fairly easy to grasp. However, I should have known that if it was easy, it probably wasn't right. Not until I left home to attend college in another state did I begin to reconsider this philosophy.

At the Christian university I attended, an amazingly wise teacher used the Bible to teach us some principles in economics. One of the principles he taught us was that it is biblical to pay taxes. That was an interesting concept to me, but I was struck by the scriptural mandate to do so and impressed with the relationship this had to respect. My professor used the scriptures found in Matthew in which Jesus says, "Give to Caesar what is Caesar's, and to God what is God's" (Matt. 22:21b NIV). He showed us how people who are put in a position of authority over us were put in that position by God, and that we are to respect the position God has put them in.

The truth of this idea really hits home and extends beyond his example. God put our parents, teachers, bosses, and government officials in the position they are in, and we are to respect them for that reason alone. Despite our affinity for someone in authority over us, we are commanded to respect them. By respecting those authorities, we are in turn respecting God, who has sovereignly placed them in their positions. Conversely, disrespecting authorities—no matter how much we dislike or disagree with them demonstrates disrespect for God.

The Bible makes several references to respect. "Each of you must respect his mother and father" (Lev. 19:3 NIV). "Rise in the presence of the aged, show respect for the elderly and revere your God" (Lev. 19:32 NIV). This notion of freely giving respect is contrary to our human nature; but it is clearly what the Bible calls us to do. Ephesians states, "Slaves obey your earthly masters with respect and fear, and with sincerity of heart just as you would obey Christ. Obey them not only to win their favor when their eye is on you, but like slaves of Christ, doing the will of God from your heart. Serve wholeheartedly, as if you were serving the Lord, not men" (Eph. 6:5–7 NIV). Peter wrote, "Slaves, submit yourselves to your masters with all respect, not only to those who are good and considerate, but also to those who are harsh" (1 Pet. 2:17 NIV). In our own society, it might be helpful to read this as, "Employees, submit yourselves to your bosses with all respect. . . ." Talk about a tough command!

Inevitably, someone will object at this point and ask, "What about the times when someone in authority asks us to do something that is contrary to what God has commanded?" In these situations, we are expected to obey God and to follow his commands, even if it means going against a person in authority over us. Even then, however, God expects us to do this in a respectful manner. Too often though, this question is just a diversion from the command to show respect to those in authority. Too often, this objection is raised in an attempt to justify a person's own inability or unwillingness to respect those in authority over them.

Human nature is selfish. We want to be first. Most people, especially in our Western culture, have a fierce independence; we want to control our own lives, our own destinies, and our own conduct. We tend to resist those who are placed above us. Yet, the Word clearly commands us to respect others. Is it tough? Many times it is. Perhaps as professionals we should keep this in mind as we govern, supervise, and direct those who have been assigned to our own areas.

As a Christian professional, do you demonstrate respect to those in authority over you? What about to those who report to you? Are you the kind of supervisor that has earned the respect of your subordinates? Has the *boomerang* of respect not come back to you because you've never sent it? If you consider yourself a servant of Christ, the practice of respect should become more and more natural as you mature in your spiritual walk with God. Respect should become one of the most natural things a Christian exercises. Respect should become a natural habit. The world is full of hurting people. Like Aretha Franklin, women cry out that all they want is a little respect. Like Rodney Dangerfield, men complain that they never get any respect. But rather than focusing upon whether or not we are respected, we should focus instead on showing respect for others. In respecting others, we will demonstrate our respect to the Lord.

4

Charity

Preserving the Dignity of Work

David W. Whitlock

Years ago, I heard a preacher tell about one of his children who had a habit of giving away everything he had. Whenever children would come to visit, his son would empty his piggybank and load his friends down with his savings. The preacher made the statement that of all his children, he prayed God would make that child rich. He explained that he prayed that prayer because that child knew how to give it away. What a refreshing attitude. I suspect that child had a deeper understanding of wealth and blessings than most adults. He seemed to understand that even if he had given away everything he had, the truth was that his daddy had more. The child was focused on how much he had. And when you're focused on what you have, instead of what you don't, you are free to give and free to share.

Most people are consumed with the opposite attitude. Get. Grab. Hoard. Keep. Our sin nature is selfish. Our old nature is stingy. Our natural inclination is to try to get more and more and more. Some going into the workforce for the first time will have the tendency to adopt that same mindset. Others going to college with the idea of getting a career instead of an education will be tempted to major in consumption and to adopt careers that provide the opportunity to grab, hoard, and keep.

The irony is that the more we get, the more we think we need. We see this tendency even in the beginning with the story of Adam and Eve. God gave Adam and Eve everything they could ever need. The whole world was theirs to enjoy. They were rich and living in paradise. But when Satan approached them, he convinced them that they should want more.

Don't you want more? Don't you want to be like God, to know good and evil? They gave in to the seduction of more. But as Adam and Eve discovered, the seduction of wanting more and more, and better and bigger is a trap. My hope is that we can readjust our thinking. The world has its standards. God's standards are different.

Jesus taught that the last shall be first. He taught that if you want to be the greatest, you must become the least, you must be a servant. In the Old Testament we read, "There is one who scatters yet increases more; and there is one who withholds more than is right, but it leads to poverty. The generous soul will be made rich, and he who waters will also be watered himself" (Prov. 11:24–25). What a contrast. The one who is generous, who gives away, will be given even more; but the one who is stingy and selfish will suffer poverty. God's ways are different than the world's ways, and God's people are different than the world. Therefore, the ways of God's people ought to stand in stark contrast to the world.

One way in which the people of God are to be different from the world in which they live has to do with work and the rewards and blessings received from our work. Our attitude about work and the blessings we receive from work is to be governed by God's laws. One illustration of this principle is found in Leviticus. Of all the books of the Bible, most people describe Leviticus as the most difficult to understand. It is probably fair to say that many have heard no sermons or at most, a handful of teachings expositing the book of Leviticus. It is filled with laws and commands that seem archaic to us and our modern lives. Many wonder what Leviticus is all about and whether it even relates to a Christian in the modern world.

The precepts of Leviticus were originally for the Israelites just after their exodus from Egypt. Camping at the base of Mount Sinai, they were molded into a nation that belonged to God, a unique nation that would be governed by God's standards, God's ways. They would be separated, different from the world around them. They would obey specific commands related to health, relationships, worship, and work. Among the laws about offerings, sacrifices, dietary laws, childbirth, diseases and health, crime and punishment, feasts, and religious ceremonies, are commands on relationships with one another, and on our moral and ethical behavior. One such principle governing the duty to provide and care for those less fortunate is taught in Leviticus. "When you reap the harvest of your land, you are not to reap to the very edge of your field or gather the gleanings of your harvest. You must not strip your vineyard bare or gather its fallen grapes. Leave them for the poor and the foreign resident; I am the LORD your God" (Lev. 19:9–10).

In this passage about sowing and reaping, we are introduced to the peculiar practice of allowing the poor, the widowed, and the stranger to gather grain in one's fields. We know this custom from the story of Ruth, who as a foreigner and a widow in Bethlehem, Judah, went into the fields to pick the missed grain from the reapers. Among the principles taught in this Levitical requirement are truths that relate to our lives as people called by Christ to be unique and different from the world around us.

First, this passage illustrates that work is a sacred responsibility. Work is good, right, and honorable. Work is required. Levitical law demanded that the owner of a field plant the whole field, but when harvest time came, the corners were to be left unharvested. They were for the poor and needy to harvest. It was a safety net for those without. Even the missed and dropped grain was to be left for the poor as well. It was a fair and equitable welfare system. But there was no command that the field's owner was required to harvest the corners of the field and then hand over the grain and the fruit to the needy. No command was given that the missed and dropped grain should be gleaned and then handed over to the poor. That would have robbed the poor of the opportunity and the dignity to work.

Many operate under the notion that society owes them something. Our own nation has, in an attempt to provide for those who are needy and poor, an entire class of dependents who have been enslaved by a perverted welfare system. I am convinced that God's Word teaches that nothing is owed to us apart from work; that apart from the infirmed and disabled, people are required to work for what they receive. While some are prevented from contributing and from working because of strange laws and unreasonable requirements, far too many have chosen or been forced not to work. This kind of attitude and decision is not to be found among the people of God. The unharvested corners of the field, and the dropped and missed grain left in the field, are a testament to the notion that one is required to work, to earn his or her own way.

However, though the totality of the Bible teaches that God does not value slothfulness and laziness, it also teaches the imperative and responsibility to give out of God's blessings. Many readily affirm the notion of work as good, honorable, and a sacred obligation. Many embrace the notion that if one does not work, one does not eat. But this passage also clearly teaches that, as God's people, we are responsible to provide for those less fortunate. The corners of our fields are to be used for the benefit of others. The corners of the fields belonging to God's people should be used to provide for the welfare of the needy and the poor.

Among the lessons we can glean from this passage in Leviticus are these: Work is honorable and ordained of God. Work allows us to participate in the blessings and rewards of God. The blessings and rewards of God are meant to be shared. Living according to God's ways results in this wonderful promise from the one true God, Jehovah, the maker of heaven and earth: "I am the Lord your God." And in Jehovah's eyes, it is our responsibility to work. Nothing is owed to us apart from work. Nothing is free, save the most important thing in the world. The only thing in life that is free is the one thing which you could never earn by work—salvation and righteousness in the sight of God. While all of our works are as filthy rags, Christ grace gives us what we cannot earn.

Believers who have trusted Jesus and surrendered their lives to Him must remind themselves that it is their responsibility to give out of God's blessings—to use the corners of their fields for the benefit of others. Besides, the truth is that Christians could give everything they have, and yet their Father in heaven still has more. God is the provider of our blessings, and believers simply cannot out-give or out-bless the Father.

Spiritual Accounting

Shelly Francka

"So if you have not been faithful with the unrighteous money, who will trust you with what is genuine? And if you have not been faithful with what belongs to someone else, who will give you what is your own? No household slave can be the slave of two masters, since either he will hate one and love the other, or he will be devoted to one and despise the other. You can't be slaves to both God and money"
(Luke 16:11–13).

In order for a balance sheet to reconcile, the following formula is used: *Total Assets minus Total Liabilities equals Stockholder's Wealth.* The Accounting Formula states: *Assets - Liabilities = Equity.* Several principles of accounting have relevance to life in general. I am reminded of a cold December afternoon. As the sun started to set, the wind picked up bringing the temperature down rather quickly. My fingers and toes started to go numb from the biting wind. The stinging numbness motivated me to exchange the bell from one hand to the other. While I tried to warm one hand, I used the other to ring the bell to a rhythm I felt appropriate for the Salvation Army. I had decided several weeks earlier that I should be a Christmas bell ringer. It was a Friday, a great way to end the week and get out of the office. I thought this would be a great way to help others but instead found my Lord helping me. The longer I stood there ringing that bell, hopping from foot to foot, greeting unfamiliar faces as they entered the grocery store, the more humbled I became.

As I stood there ringing, I noticed that the elderly and those who appeared to have the least gave the most. I watched as a woman pulled up in a 1970 era Pontiac Bonneville. You could hear the engine sputtering and coughing as it came to a rolling stop, relieved to have made it this far. The vehicle had holes in the body of the car from the years of rust slowly eating away the color and the metal. The door opened and out stepped an elderly woman in her late seventies. Her well-worn jacket and shoes were old and dirty, and she had an unkempt look about her. She greeted me, slowly reached into her pocketbook, and pulled out a five-dollar bill. As I thanked her and wished her a Merry Christmas, she simply smiled and slowly proceeded into the store.

A few minutes later a woman in her late forties pulled up in a new Ford Explorer, which appeared never to have wintered the harsh elements of December. As the woman got out of her vehicle, I could see that her nails were well manicured, she was supporting a very large diamond on her wedding ring, and she was wearing very expensive looking shoes. It was my practice to greet everyone who entered the store with a "Merry Christmas," "God bless you, thank you." This particular woman looked at me, gave me a once over, and then proceeded into the store. She never acknowledged me, smiled, or muttered a word. It was as if she simply chose to look through the Salvation Army Donation Kettle. She appeared to ignore me, ignore the ringing of the bell, and ignore the need of those less fortunate.

I found myself trying to justify her behavior. Was it too cold for her? Was she in a hurry? Did she not have any change? Maybe she would give a little change after she paid for her groceries. Unfortunately, this woman was not an isolated case. The longer I stood there, the more ashamed I became. I was ashamed of my own behavior as well as the behavior of those who ignored the opportunity to help others in need during the Christmas season. Some appeared to be in too much of a hurry to get in out of the cold to take time to drop a few coins into the little red bucket. During my stint as a bell ringer, some stated that they didn't have the cash on them. But one man walked up, filthy and appearing not to have showered for days, smiled in regret as he handed me thirty cents. His face showed embarrassment as he simply stated, "This is all I have." He gave everything. I felt the Lord smile down on him and prayed that God would bless him abundantly. How many times had I walked by a Salvation Army bucket thinking that I didn't want to give because I had just given earlier that day or at a different store? How much did I think was enough? I felt the guilt starting to expand inside my heart. If I had given during those opportunities, maybe only one dollar a day for the month of December, I would have given around thirty dollars. That amount would be almost nothing, a tank of gas, what I spend on soda each month, a dinner out with my husband. How many times have I walked by, ignoring others, ignoring those less fortunate than I, and giving nothing?

As Christians, do we ignore the Salvation Army buckets, the food banks, our neighbors, others in our communities that struggle to feed their families? Luke 16:1–13 tells us that we need to be good managers of our money and the money of other people no matter how insignificant it may be. While our money on earth may buy us material luxuries, true riches await us in heaven. If we are frugal with our charity, our mercy, and our kindness, then how will God trust us with the riches of heaven?

Consider the exchange between a young man and Jesus. When the young man asked Jesus which of the commandments was the most important, Jesus responded by quoting the Old Testament. "The most important one is this: "Listen, Israel: The LORD our God, the LORD is One. Love the LORD your God with all your heart, with all your soul, and with all your strength" (Deut. 6:4–5). The second is this: "Do not take revenge or bear a grudge against members of your community, but love your neighbor as yourself; I am the LORD" (Lev. 19:18).

The man responded by saying "'You are right, Teacher! You have correctly said that He is One, and there is no one else except Him. And to love Him with all your heart, with all your understanding, and with all your strength, and to love your neighbor as yourself, is far more [important] than all the burnt offerings and sacrifices.' When Jesus saw that he answered intelligently, He said to him, 'You are not far from the kingdom of God.' And no one dared to question Him any longer" (Mark 12:32–34).

We cannot serve two masters. To be in this world and not of this world is challenging. In order to appear successful, we are measured by our income, our mortgage payment, and the type of vehicle we drive. However, instead of using worldly goods as a measure of success, what if every financial decision was based upon how pleasing it would be to God. Instead of coveting our money to buy bigger and better, what if we helped others become successful? Proverbs states, "The sluggard's craving will be the death of him, because his hands refuse to work. All day long he craves for more, but the righteous give without sparing" (Prov. 21:25, 26). Those who are close to God give without being tightfisted. They are generous to those around them, not just to friends and family, but to complete strangers.

Jesus promotes unselfishness when he states, "Then Jesus said to his host, 'When you give a luncheon or dinner, do not invite your friends, your brothers or relatives, or your rich neighbors; if you do, they may invite you back and so you will be repaid. But when you give a banquet, invite the poor, the crippled, the lame, the blind, and you will be blessed. Although they cannot repay you, you will be repaid at the resurrection of the righteous'" (Luke 14:12–14). Humility and unselfishness are among Christ's most endearing attributes. He unselfishly humbled himself as a man. He humbled himself even unto the cross where he paid our account in full. He does not send us a reminder telling us that we still have a balance due. His sacrifice paid our debt in full, and he showers us with unmerited grace. His blood, credited to our account, leaves a zero balance. His righteousness inspires us to give selflessly to our neighbors and strangers.

As an example of pure love, Jesus paid all our debts and offers the advice that in order to draw closer to God, we need to be giving, loving, forgiving, and merciful. God has shown us great mercy, and we should show others the same mercy. We were bought and paid for with the blood of Christ. Those with managerial, executive, or fiduciary roles should have constant fidelity within those positions as they manage or supervise the assets of others. Maintaining a lifestyle of serving God while being a slave to riches is neither possible nor desirable.

While the accounting formula states: *Assets - Liabilities = Equity,* perhaps as Christians we should use the following Spiritual Account Balancing formula: *Worldly Assets + Liability to Love = Charity toward Others.* When we take our assets or worldly possessions and we show mercy, favor, benevolence, the result will be our cheerful charity toward those others, particularly toward those most needy around us. Standing in right relationship with God can produce no less. Instead of using the accounting balance sheet formula, *Total Assets minus Total Liabilities equals Shareholder's Wealth,* perhaps we ought to minimize our liabilities by increasing our charity. We know that every spiritual debt we have has been paid in full by Christ. *Christ's righteousness + Faith = our Eternal Life (our wealth and riches in glory!).* Talk about shareholder's wealth!

In other accounting terms, we are told that Christ's righteousness was imputed to our account. Through faith, we are credited with His right-standing with God. "But to him that worketh not, but believeth on him that justifieth the ungodly, his faith is counted for righteousness. Even as David also describeth the blessedness of the man, unto whom God imputeth righteousness without works, saying, 'Blessed are they whose iniquities are forgiven, and whose sins are covered. Blessed is the man to whom the Lord will not impute sin'" (Rom. 4:5–8 KJV). Through faith, Christ's righteousness is literally credited to our account!

Our brief life on earth is a period of preparation for eternity in heaven. Redemption from sin and the call to a holy life are never earned but graciously given by God's unmerited grace. As Christians we can make no claim upon God's grace by fulfilling what is our duty. But the Apostle James reminds us that faith without works is dead. And Paul's first letter to the Corinthians proclaims that our works apart from love are mere noise and activity. We know we cannot serve both God and money. And we know we are blessed in order that we may bless others. This knowledge results in a godly desire and obligation to show charity toward others—to apply our Spiritual Account Balancing formula: *Worldly Assets + Liability to Love = Charity toward Others.* Our duty is to serve God and others, to become His disciples, to demonstrate His love by putting into practice His attributes of mercy, kindness and charity toward others.

5

Faithfulness

A Picture of Faithfulness

Rodney Reeves

FAITHFULNESS IS one of those words we all use but have a hard time defining. We think we know what we mean when we say, "He's a faithful guy," or "She's a faithful friend." But what we really mean is that he's reliable or she's loyal—but these qualities are not the same as faithfulness. Reliability could be a function of habit; loyalty often involves shared interests. Faithfulness derives from something more. The Pharisees were reliable. They fasted twice a week, prayed twice per day. The twelve were loyal to Jesus. They followed him wherever he went (except to the cross!). But, when we consider the gospel story, few would describe either group as faithful. This is why I think some of us are confused about what it means to be faithful to God.

Sadly, some may think of faithfulness as a bribe, a *quid pro quo* arrangement with God. "I will do what He wants of me so that He will do what I want of Him." In this case, faithfulness degenerates to a form of manipulation, where we try to bend God to our will, placating Him with acts of obeisance. We count on an all-seeing, all-knowing God to repay us for services rendered. Obedience is necessity. Compliance is strategy. Like spoiled children, we think we've figured out the game of reward. Like opportunistic employees, we know how to work the system. In this unholy role reversal, God becomes our debtor. We make demands. So, we open our hands as we bend our knee.

Others prefer to speak of faithfulness as an investment strategy. Doing the right thing is a practical matter. Sin has its consequences. Wickedness leads to misery. Fools persist in such destructive behavior. Only the wise are prosperous. So, the faithful look for dividends in clean living as we point out the downside of a reckless life. We see how the vacuous pursuit of selfishness turns restless seekers into narcissistic consumers. We know immediate gratification never satisfies. So in defiant obedience, we sneer at the shortsighted foolishness of those who waste their lives on wanton pleasures. "Yeah, they may look like they're having fun; but, deep down, they must be miserable." Trying to convince ourselves, we repeat the mantra: faithfulness requires patience. We count on the fact that evil catches up with rebels. What goes around comes around. Righteousness will bring its own rewards. Eventually, everyone will get what they deserve.

But, what happens when the wicked die at a ripe old age, enjoying their worldly vices till the end? What do we say when faithfulness to God *doesn't* pay, when God doesn't keep his end of our bargain? Why do bad things happen to good people? Indeed, after considering the injustices that accompany our so-called "faithfulness," some may resonate with the Preacher who said, "I have seen everything during my lifetime of futility; there is a righteous man who perishes in his righteousness, and there is a wicked man who prolongs his life in his wickedness. Do not be excessively righteous, and do not be overly wise. Why should you ruin yourself?" (Eccl. 7:15–16 NASB).

If doing the right thing makes a difference, why doesn't God reward the faithful for making a difference? Shouldn't a faithful life curry the favor of God? We know God loves all people, but shouldn't He love us more? Some may be tempted to join the chorus of the priests who said, "It is vain to serve God. What do we profit by keeping his command or by going about as mourners before the Lord of hosts? Now we count the arrogant happy; evildoers not only prosper, but when they put God to test they escape" (Mal. 3:14–15 NRSV).

This is why I like the way the Psalmist describes the faithful as those who "stand by their oath even to their hurt" (Ps. 15:4 NRSV). Faithfulness is not a matter of doing the right thing so that we may gain an advantage with God. In fact, when I consider the faithful (especially the heroes of the Bible), it has become ever more apparent to me that the obedient rarely got what they deserved. The prophets were murdered. Jesus was crucified. Paul was imprisoned. John was exiled. Where's the justice, the payoff, the reward? Why did God let this happen, over and over again? Suffering and death are not very appetizing carrots to dangle in front of sons and daughters of heaven. Who would be faithful for that? Only those who know what faithfulness is: to be faithful is to be full of faith.

Faithful sons and daughters are full of faith. They trust completely. They believe thoroughly. They have faith no matter what. And, what do they believe? Not only do they believe that God turns evil into good (Gen. 50:20; Rom. 8:28) and that history has a divine purpose (Jer. 29:11; Eph. 1:9–11). The faithful believe the gospel of Jesus is the story that must be played out in the lives of every follower of Christ. The death, burial, and resurrection of Christ is the predestined life of those who belong to Christ. The cross was no accident. Easter is no *plan B*. God wasn't working "on the fly" when He built the temple we call "salvation." In fact, the gospel is what God had planned all along—not only how He would save us when we died, but also how He saves us as we live. Paul called it being "crucified with Christ" (Gal. 2:2). For him, the gospel was a *pattern* to follow (Phil. 3:17), a life to be imitated (1 Cor. 11:1)—to see things like he saw them: "have this mindset among yourselves which was also in Christ Jesus" (Phil. 2:5[1]). How did Jesus and Paul see life the same way?

Paul believed what happened to Jesus would also happen to him, to Timothy, to Epaphroditus, to all of his converts. It's a story of humiliation leading to exaltation, death producing life, shame morphing into honor, loss reckoned as gain, weakness becoming strength. This is not giving to get. This is giving up. Paul realized "the world has been crucified to me, and I to the world" (Gal. 6:14 NASB). This is why, when Paul experienced *bad things*, he believed he was receiving the grace of God (2 Cor. 11:24—12:10). Imprisonment did not impede the gospel—who can chain the good news of Christ (Phil. 1:12–18)? Waiting for his Roman trial, Paul saw his imprisonment as a confirmation of the gospel. His chains proved he was imitating

1. Author's translation.

Christ; what happened to Paul is what happened to Jesus (Phil. 2:7–8; 3:8–10). Live the gospel and Jewish leaders will beat you, Roman rulers will kill you. The veil of the temple was ripped in half; every knee will bow to Christ (not Caesar!). This is the way it's supposed to be—it is predestined. It's what Paul believed. And, because he was full of this faith, he endured all things, longing to know the "power of His resurrection and the fellowship of His sufferings, being conformed to His death" (Phil. 3:10 NASB). Paul believed bearing the cross of Christ would mean his resurrection. Totally.

Can you imagine how frustrating it must have been for Paul's opponents? Like Job's counselors, they must have interpreted the horrible things that happened to Paul as God's just punishment. The way they saw it, God couldn't get it through Paul's thick skull that He wasn't pleased with the rebel apostle who shared table with Gentiles, ate pork, and worshipped God on the wrong day (Sunday!). Beaten and humiliated, shipwrecked (who controls the wind and the sea?) and imprisoned, nothing could stop him. Paul fully believed he was on a mission for Christ: not only to tell the good news, but to *be* the good news. This is why whenever a cross was placed on the back of the apostle, he embraced it with the passionate kiss of his life. For him, a crucified life was the only way to live.

So, this is faithfulness. Believing God no matter the circumstances. Doing the right thing simply because it's right. Knowing bad things will happen to good people. Denying the ways of the world. Seeing the gospel as a way of life. Reckoning loss as gain, humility as honorable, sacrifice as blessing, weakness as strength. Indeed, if the world has been crucified to us, and we to the world, then everything is upside down. Even though the world says, "Get ahead by promoting yourself," we will promote others because the things of this world don't matter. Even though the world says, "Get what you can while you can," we will be spent for Christ because He was spent for us. Even though the world says, "create your own destiny," we will be conformed to the image of God's Son. For, when it's all said and done, Jesus is what faithfulness looks like.

6

Truthfulness

To Tell the Truth

Marinell Rayfield Erven

As parents, my husband and I tried to instill the value of truthfulness in our children from an early age. Both of us were well into our professional lives when our children were born, and we were in agreement that *truth* was a critical issue. We both had witnessed the ill effects that resulted from lying, and we were determined to instill truthfulness as a strong character trait in our children. As our children grew older, we were amazed at the many variances in truth that not only would confront them, but that they would use in challenging us. At this point, I began to think more and more about *truth* as I realized I had become a walking and talking mentor for my children. Living in truth and modeling truth seemed very different. The former was done without much thought; the latter required active thought on every level.

Many times, I have personally reflected on whether I consistently tell—as the courts would say—"the truth, the whole truth, and nothing but the truth." Or, I ask myself, do I tend to modify the truth depending on the situation? As a child, my mother frowned upon the *little white lies* that I had believed were reasonable. However, I have found that as an adult I still have that innate ability to stretch, distort, minimize, or even diminish truthfulness. I've found that in critical situations, these little distortions are relatively painless. However, the more distortion I spin, the more painful is the experience.

As one intrigued with language, I routinely decorated my place of work by mounting posters with inspirational, critical thinking, or humorous quotes. My all-time favorite is, "The truth will set you free, but first it will make you miserable." This quote rang true at so many levels throughout my life. At the most basic level, I thought of my soul in relationship to that quote. I remember when God made me realize that even though I had attended every church service and been active in church youth activities all my life, the truth was that I really didn't have a personal relationship with him. I had been going through all the motions for years, but I didn't have that peace in my heart that assured me I would have a home in heaven. I was miserable! Like Jacob, I wrestled with God. I lacked the peace of knowing him personally. Fear gripped me until finally God spoke peace to my troubled heart, and I suddenly had that peace that passes all understanding. That peace was truth—salvation—the very truth for which God allowed his Son to die. Reaching that truth was painful.

In our daily lives, I wonder how often we resort to something less than the truth. I remember driving my daughter, Tiffany, home after kindergarten one day. She was telling me that a student had asked her if she liked a treat another little girl had given her that day. Our daughter had truthfully told her no. Straight truth was what Tiffany gave. I suggested that she might answer more tactfully. But it caused me to think of my own willingness to tell the whole truth. How many times have you been asked, "Does this make me look fat?" I know how I probably would have answered. Should I be truthful and tell my lunch mate that I don't really like the food at the restaurant she chose? When a friend from church visits our home and we say grace over our meal, even though we neglect prayer of a quick sandwich when we are alone, are we being truthful? How truthful am I? Is it possible to be truthful, while being kind and tactful? Or do I resort to those proverbial little white lies in order simply to avoid having to confront the truth?

Colossians tells us, "Lie not one to another, seeing that you have put off the old man with his deeds" (Col. 3:9 KJV). I'm convinced that this verse should be applied literally. Paul was telling those who are saved to renounce their old ways, and that included putting aside deceitfulness. He desired them to embrace honesty and integrity. Jesus had already stated, "I am the truth" (John 14:6 NIV). Believing Christ means following his example. The more the Colossians patterned themselves after Jesus, the more truthful and the more like Him they would become. The same is true for us. As we pattern ourselves after Christ, we will naturally become more like him, including becoming more and more truthful and consistent.

In the parable of the two sons in Matthew 21, we see one son who told his master he would not work but later repented and did work. The second son said that he would but then did not. When Jesus asked which of them had done the father's will, the answer was the first. I imagine that there likely was some suffering on the part of the first son before he repented and obeyed his father. However, the second son's mind was probably consumed, as ours would be, with rationalizing his lie. Like this son, once we lie, we pacify ourselves with flawed reasoning to assuage our guilt. The more practiced we become, the more and more calloused to genuine truth become our hearts and consciences.

Anthropologist Margaret Meade once said, "What people say, what people do, and what they say they do are entirely different things." Sadly, this is evident in far too many members of our society. We work with them. We socialize with them. And, let's be truthful, we worship with them. What is even sadder, we *are* they! None of us would want to return to barbarian ways and have our tongues cut out if we told a lie. But with such a penalty looming over me, I must confess that I might find it more expedient to tell the truth.

God wants his children to tell the truth—to be the truth. It is worth our time to make a concentrated effort to speak in the spirit of truth at all times. Does this mean to say literally everything we think, believe, or want in every situation? Zechariah states, "These are the things you must do: Speak truth to one another; render honest and peaceful judgments in your gates" (Zech. 8:16 KJV). We, therefore, should strive not only for truthfulness but also for peace. It is possible to be a kind and gentle teller of truth. Our words should not belittle, disparage, or cause harm. Such harmful words would not result in peaceful co-existence in our gates.

Whether before our children or our coworkers, truthfulness should be our guiding force. Though we may have to struggle against shading the truth, telling only half-truths or white lies, God's expectation is truthfulness. "So Jesus said to the Jews who had believed Him, "If you continue in My word, you really are My disciples. You will know the truth, and the truth will set you free" (John 8:31–33 KJV). Jesus Himself is Truth. "Jesus told him, 'I am the way, the truth, and the life'" (John 14:6a KJV). As we are to be conformed to his image, so ought we to be people of our word, true and faithful witnesses, and the kind of people others know will tell the truth.

7

Humility

Humility in Attitude and Action

Rodger W. Minatra

"Do nothing out of rivalry or conceit, but in humility consider others as more important than yourselves. Everyone should look out not only for his own interests but also for the interests of others" (Phil. 2:3–4). In the eulogy for President Reagan, the elder President Bush told the story of how not long after Reagan's surgery, which repaired the wounds he received in the assassination attempt on his life, his aides entered his hospital room and found him on his hands and knees. Worried that his nurse would get in trouble, President Reagan was cleaning up a water spill from the floor—an act of humility and character by a person of considered position and power. Such an action seems counter to our present culture. More times than not, our culture tells us that meekness is weakness, compassion is compromise, and submission is suicide. Humility is certainly not one of the praised character traits on Donald Trump's hit program, *The Apprentice*.

In a day and age when the use of the word *competition* is only outdone by the word *globalization*, it seems difficult to find a place for the word *humility*, especially in the world of business. Humility, defined as the condition of being humble, is often associated with meekness, submission, lowly rank or position, and self abasement. If this is humility, how can a Christian succeed in a world that seems to reward pride and aggressiveness?

The Bible tells us that humility is necessary for success. King Solomon, considered one of the richest and wisest men ever to live, addresses humility several times in the book of Proverbs. "The fear of the LORD is Wisdom's instruction, and humility comes before honor" (Prov. 15:33). "Before his downfall, a man's heart is proud, but before honor comes humility" (Prov. 18:12). "The result of humility is fear of the LORD, along with wealth, honor, and life" (Prov. 22:4). "Better to be lowly of spirit with the humble, than to divide plunder with the proud" (Prov. 16:19). "A person's pride will humble him, but a humble spirit will gain honor" (Prov. 29:23).

In each of these verses, humility precedes honor; and in one, it precedes wealth and life. All of these are included measurements in the sense of worldly success. The Bible also tells us that humility is part of the character of Christ Jesus. As Christians we measure our success by our Christlike character. Jesus himself encourages us to follow His example and take on the character of gentleness and humility. "Come to Me, all of you who are weary and burdened, and I will give you rest. All of you, take up My yoke and learn from Me, because I am gentle and humble in heart, and you will find rest for yourselves, For My yoke is easy and My burden is light" (Matt. 11:28–30).

In Christian circles, humility is often defined as avoiding false pride about our abilities or accomplishments. However, a deeper knowledge of the Christian faith informs that humility is more than refraining from bragging or boasting about our accomplishments. Scripture tells us to think of others as better than ourselves. I have often struggled with this verse but have come to believe that humility is the realization that I cannot live in a sinful world and expect to accomplish anything good apart from God. William Wilberforce, credited with the abolition of slavery in Europe, wrote in his book *Real Christianity* (published in 1797), that our inability is our great asset; it creates a humility that becomes dependent on God's grace working in us. Likewise, in 1 Corinthians, the Apostle Paul tells us that knowledge without humility leads to intellectual vanity.

Scripture also tells us that humility is both an attitude and action of obedience. "Make your own attitude that of Christ Jesus, who, existing in the form of God, did not consider equality with God as something to be used for His own advantage. Instead He emptied Himself by assuming the form of a slave, taking on the likeness of men. And when He had come as a man in His external form, He humbled Himself by becoming obedient to the point of death—even the death on a cross" (Phil. 2:5–8).

When I think of humility as an attitude and not just an action, it brings to mind a statement I read several years ago. Ethel Barrett, known as *The Story Lady*, was one of the most popular Christian personalities in America during the mid-twentieth century. She said, "Humility has its own form of pride." Growing up in a Christian family I was taught the importance of humility, and I've practiced it. Unfortunately, an anxious heart and a prideful desire can rob the most humble actions of their honor. "Humble yourselves therefore under the mighty hand of God, so that He may exalt you in due time, casting all your care upon Him, because He cares about you" (1 Pet. 5:6–7).

Humility is tough. It goes against the grain. We naturally tend toward being served rather than serving others. But a Christian ought to follow the example of our Lord who humbled Himself. Christian professionals should be the kind of people who never think so highly of themselves that they are unwilling to put others' needs ahead of their own or are unwilling to serve others. Christian professionals should be the type of people who, no matter what elevated station in life they may enjoy, might be found on their hands and knees mopping up a spill to spare someone else trouble.

8

Perseverance

What Keeps You Going?

R. Stanton Norman

ONLY TWO men failed to return from the storied Lewis and Clark expedition of the early 1800s.[1] One man failed to return because he got sick and died. The other man failed to return because he was smitten. He had just seen the breadth and length of what would one day become the United States of America—from the Great Plains to the Rockies to the Columbia basin of Oregon to the Pacific Ocean. The vast wonders of the continent had a grip on his soul. So when Lewis and Clark set out for home, John Colter waved them goodbye. He stayed behind to explore the wide lands that were outside the scope of the expedition. He wanted to follow some of those trails and paddle up some of those rivers he had passed by on the way to the Pacific. Their wild beauty haunted him.

Colter trapped beaver in the virgin streams of the high country. He was the first white man to witness the geysers of Yellowstone. The young man's love affair with uncharted lands kept him in constant danger. Close encounters with monster grizzlies, churning whitewater rapids, and always dangerous Indians tested his courage, pluck and reflexes. As years went by, he gained a legendary status among his fellow trappers and mountain men—men not easily impressed. But the accomplishment that sealed Colter's reputation as a living legend was not a battle with a grizzly, shooting rapids in a fragile canoe, or scaling an unknown mountain range.

1. The following account of John Colter is excerpted from the work, Steve Farrar, *Finishing Strong: Going the Distance for Your Family* (Sisters, OR: Multnomah Pub., 2000).

John Colter was best known for a single foot race. The account of the race would be told and retold around campfires from the Columbia to the Missouri. John Colter ran like few men in history had ever run; he was running for his life. Colter had been trapping beaver in a particular stream with an old friend from the Lewis and Clark expedition, John Potts. As they were canoeing down a stretch of river not far from what is today Bozeman, Montana, they heard a rustling in the brush on both sides of the riverbank. In the next instant, the two men were surrounded by Blackfeet Indians with drawn bows.

With no time for escape downstream, Colter did the only thing he could have done; he headed for the bank. As they were getting out of the canoe, a large Blackfeet brave ran forward and snatched the rifle out of the hands of John Potts. Colter, a man of great physical strength and courage, knew that any sign of fear would only ensure their torturous death at the hands of these Blackfeet Indians. The desperate trapper grabbed the rifle and wrestled it away from the Indian, throwing the man to the ground in the process. Colter tossed the weapon to Potts and turned to confront the startled warriors.

Potts had seen enough and jumped into the canoe to make a getaway. "No!" shouted Colter, knowing there was no escape in that direction. Arrows rained into the canoe, killing Potts. The river current swept the canoe and the body of Colter's friend downstream. Colter himself stood on the bank, unarmed and alone. The Blackfeet swarmed around him, stripped him naked, and then tied him down as they tried to determine what to do with him.

Some warriors shouted, "Skin him alive!" Others cried, "Beat him to death!" Still other braves roared, "Burn him alive!" Then one of the Blackfeet offered a creative idea. The chief approached Colter and asked him if he could run like a deer. Colter indicated that he was not as fast as a deer, but slow like a turtle. This was a lie, for Colter was a remarkably fast runner. The chief, however, took the bait and quickly led everyone to a nearby sandy plain. He made a mark in the ground, and his warriors toed the line. He then took Colter and gave him a three hundred-yard head start. The buck-naked Colter took off like a shot. Except for moccasins and loin cloths, the pursuing

Blackfeet were as naked as Colter. Each warrior also carried his favorite weapon and yearned for the honor of killing the white trapper.

The plain stretched ahead of Colter for six miles, dotted only by sagebrush and prickly pear. Shimmering on the horizon, however, Colter could see a line of trees on what must have been a bend of the river. John Colter focused on those trees and began the run of this life. Colter's bare feet were soon cut to bloody ribbons by sharp stones and prickly pear, but in this race there was no stopping. One mile passed. Two miles sped by. At approximately three miles, Colter looked back over his shoulder, for he could no longer hear the yelling of his pursuers or the slap of their moccasins in the dust. Only a handful of pursuers were still in the hunt, and they were a good distance away. One solitary brave, however, had closed to within two hundred yards. Colter's body was so stressed from the exertion of the chase that blood trickled from his mouth and nose.

At four miles, Colter looked back again. With protective moccasins on his feet, the Blackfeet brave had gained a lot of ground and was less than fifty yards away. Colter knew his broad, naked back was in range of the warrior's sharp lance. So, without any warning, the hunted man suddenly whirled and stopped. Colter faced the onrushing Indian and threw his hands up in the air as if to surrender. The shocked brave immediately threw his lance and stumbled head over heels as the weapon left his hand. The lance fell short, and Colter rushed and snatched it from the place where it landed. He then took the weapon and plunged it into his pursuer before the exhausted warrior could regain his footing. Colter drove the lance into his pursuers body with such force that the man was penned to the ground to die by his own weapon.

Summoning every ounce of strength he had left, Colter ran the remaining mile or so to the river and the stand of timber. A sandbar was in the middle of the stream, and at the head of this small island was a large raft of driftwood that had come down with the spring floods. Colter swam out to the raft, dove beneath it, and came up where several of the entangled logs formed a roof above his head. Here he waited for the pursuing Blackfeet, up to his neck in the icy waters under this makeshift shelter.

Colter soon heard the approaching Blackfeet. They swarmed around the river, onto the sandbar, and even stood upon the logs that covered his head. The enraged Indians could not, however, find him. The day was young, and his pursuers were anxious to avenge the death of their fallen comrade. The Blackfeet warriors kept up the hunt until late afternoon before finally withdrawing. Under the cover of darkness, John Colter swam downstream until he found a tiny stretch of bank concealed by trees and brush. Naked, half-frozen, and nearly delirious from exposure and loss of blood, Colter pulled himself out of the stream and lay gasping on the bank. He had no rifle, no food, no fire, no horse, no shoes, and no clothing. He had been stripped of everything he had but his will to live. John Colter was half-dead and 150 miles from the trading post at Bighorn. Seven days later, he walked naked, bleeding, and hungry into the Bighorn compound. In that moment, a living legend was born. Stripped of everything and against the worst odds imaginable, John Colter outran and outsmarted the pursuing Blackfeet for 156 miles. In spite of his circumstances, John Colter managed to persevere when many would have quit.

I must admit that there are days when certain aspects of this story resonate with me. For example, like Colter, I find myself in a "race" (life often has prolonged moments comparable to a marathon) not of my own choosing. Like Colter, the circumstances of my life's race are often unpleasant, uncomfortable, and even painful. In the race of life, however, there is no stopping for personal pain or discomfort. Like Colter, there are days when the circumstances of life seem to pursue and hound me; and on occasion these people, events, or circumstances of life threaten to overwhelm me and derail me in my journey.

What keeps you going when you want to quit? What keeps you in the race of life, even when every aspect of life (people, events, circumstances, etc.) would justify stopping and quitting? What keeps you going when every fiber of your being seems to scream "Stop!"? The pain is too great. The circumstances are unbearable. How do you persist, or persevere, through this journey called life?

Fortunately for us, the Bible contains the accounts of the great men and women, or heroes, of the Christian faith. We find in their lives examples of the power of God sustaining them in the midst of their "race of life." In these biblical accounts, God reveals to us how he empowered and equipped these people to continue and finish their race until completion, even when their circumstances seemed to justify quitting. Although we could profitably focus on many candidates, I want to examine the life of an Old Testament saint named Caleb. His life is a model of perseverance. Although the circumstances of his life seemed insurmountable, God sustained and enabled Caleb to persevere in his walk of faith. In fact, because Caleb faithfully persevered, we can conclude that the end of his life was better than the beginning. I am confident that the power of God that sustained Caleb will likewise equip us to continue when we would rather stop. In Josh. 14:6–14, we see the power of God motivating and sustaining Caleb over the course of a long life. Caleb persevered faithfully in the calling and tasks that God placed upon his life. What kept Caleb going? Caleb's perseverance in his life's mission was due to the faithfulness of God. These verses contain four primary lessons worth our attention.

Perseverance Is Grounded Upon the Faithfulness of God to his Word and Promises. The first lesson illustrated in this passage is that perseverance in faithful service to God rests upon the certainty, or truthfulness, of the word of God. Perseverance is directly tied to the faithfulness of God. If we believe that God cannot or will not be faithful to His promises, our certainty to persevere in life is destroyed. If we believe God cannot be trusted to speak a truthful word, we have no basis to determine truth from falsehood, right from wrong. The conviction of Caleb to claim his inheritance is grounded upon his belief that God speaks truth and, therefore, will keep His promise to him. As believers, we also can find stability and direction for our life of faith when we embrace the truth of and live in the conviction that God can be trusted to keep His word. When God declares that he will keep and sustain us (John 10:13; Rom. 8:31–39), he can be absolutely trusted to keep his promise. We can, therefore, draw strength from his promises and continue in our lives of discipleship when the occasions and circumstances of our lives threaten to derail our journey. Always remember that the God who is all powerful and all truthful will be faithful to keep His promises to us.

The Faithfulness of God to His Word and Promises Elevates Our Perspective in Life. The second lesson illustrated by this passage involving Caleb is that perspective is a powerful, determining factor for life and is derived from a right conviction regarding the word of God. Perspective is also directly connected to our ability to persevere. The gracious gift of perseverance rests upon the action of the Holy Spirit working in the life of the believer to change how that individual views his or her life and mission. Evidence of a *persevering perspective* is seen in Caleb's temporal assessment of God faithfulness. Caleb's future confidence in the empowerment of God rested upon the past and present faithfulness of God. Caleb believed God would equip him to take his inheritance because he had learned to trust God in past and present conditions. In this sense, a *persevering perspective* transforms our ability to view our past, present, and future in light of the faithfulness of God.

A *persevering perspective* also changes the way we assess our current situation. When we consider Caleb, we might be prone to see a man who was beyond the ability to accomplish his mission to take his inheritance. He was, after all, an elderly man, even by the standards of his day. "As you see, the Lord has kept me alive 45 years as He promised, since the Lord spoke this word to Moses while Israel was journeying in the wilderness. Here I am today, 85 years old" (Josh. 14:10). He would have been considered well beyond his physical prime and, therefore, unable to engage and sustain a military campaign. Whereas his contemporaries saw an old man, Caleb believed himself still fit for service and mission. Caleb believed that he was prepared and ready to accomplish his mission.

The faithfulness of God to His word and promises instills within us a perspective to persist. The persevering work of God changed the way Caleb viewed himself and his ability to fulfill the will of God for his life. He did not see himself as an aged man ready to rest in life. He viewed himself as a warrior ready to battle for his inheritance. The persevering work of God will change how we see ourselves and the circumstances of our life. A *persevering perspective* is one means by which God empowers us such that we believe and do overcome those difficulties and dilemmas. We assess problems differently. We view our calling in life differently. We interpret our ability to succeed in life differently. The gracious work of perseverance therefore transforms our perspective of ourselves, our world, and our mission in the world. Godly success will only come to those who look at life through the eyes of a persevering perspective.

The Faithfulness of God to His Word and Promises Sustains Us in Times of Great Waiting. A third lesson found in the passage about Caleb is that the faithfulness of God to His word and promises not only instilled within Caleb a persevering perspective, God's faithfulness also sustained him through a time of significant waiting. Caleb's reward came, but it was a delayed reward. He was consigned to wait for an entire generation of unfaithful Hebrews to die in the wilderness before he could enter the land of promise. Caleb waited forty years before his feet ever entered the land, and he then waited an additional five years before receiving his inheritance.

The concept of a sustained wait is quite foreign to our culture. In our world of instant gratification, delayed reward seems at best, an unfair act, or at worst, an unjust punishment. A period of prolonged, sustained waiting is perceived as cruel. What kept Caleb going each day in the wilderness as he waited for the fulfillment of the judgment of God? What sustained him? What would sustain us in a period of great waiting? The faithfulness of God works within us a perseverance that sustains us in times of great waiting. Sometimes the timing of God is immediate and instantaneous. The Bible contains numerous examples of the quick, direct intervention of God. But the Bible also contains numerous examples where the intervention of God in an event or the fulfillment of God to a promise requires a lifetime of waiting. These periods of sustained waiting seem to me to be more normative than the occasional immediate interventions of God. God graciously works in the lives of believers to bring about a perseverance that sustains us through those prolonged periods of trial and difficulty. When our lives are grounded upon the faithful God, we can endure times of great waiting. The reality of the faithfulness of

God is greater than the reality of the trying, difficult times of life in which we often find ourselves.

The Faithfulness of God to His Word and Promises Empowers Us To Confront the Major Obstacles of Life. The final truth regarding perseverance that we can glean from this passage is that the faithfulness of God to His word and promises empowers us to confront the major obstacles of life. One of the major barriers to the entrance of the Israelites into the Promised Land was their concern about "the giants of the land." The presence of giants in the land caused great fear among the covenant community. In fact, the presence of these large warrior people appears to be a major reason why the majority of Israelites refused to enter the land. The resulting distrust in the faithfulness of God to his promise that he would give the land to the Israelites was the basis for the judgment of God against them. This pronouncement is found in Numbers: "Yes, as surely as I live . . . none of the men who have seen my glory and the signs I performed in Egypt will ever see the land I swore to give their fathers. None of those who despised Me will see it" (Num. 14:21ff). Caleb believed in the promises of God, however, and did not waver in his conviction that the Israelites could take the land in the power of God. Because of his faithful belief in the promise of God, God rewarded Caleb. "Since my servant Caleb has a different spirit and followed Me completely, I will bring him into the land where he has gone, and his descendants will inherit it" (Num. 14:24).

Caleb persevered in the promises of God, and the account of the reception of his reward is recorded in Josh. 14:13–14. Caleb further demonstrated his trust in God by requesting the land occupied by the *giants* of the lands, the Anakites. This biblical text connects the ability to persevere with the ability to confront and overcome the obstacles of life. The reality of the faithfulness of God shapes and supports our ability to persevere in the course of life, even when great obstacles and barriers appear to impede our path. Sometimes God will equip us to conquer "the giants" of our lives. Sometimes God will equip to continue to wait until he removes the *giants* of our lives. In either of these cases, God will work in us in such a way that we can successfully persevere through life.

Conclusion: The writer of Ecclesiastes stated: "The end of a matter is better than its beginning; a patient spirit is better than a proud spirit" (Eccl. 7:8). This verse underscores the truth that how we conclude the race of our life is more important than how we begin that race. As one preacher once remarked, "In the Christian life, how you finish is more important than how you start." Caleb models the importance of this biblical truth. The Christian life is one marked by perseverance. In His grace and mercy, God provides His Holy Spirit to instill and work within each believer the disposition of perseverance. Perseverance, thereby, becomes one of the tenets, or fruits, that distinguishes us as regenerate children of God. The work of God whereby he sustains and equips the believer to finish the race of life is called perseverance. Like John Colter we persist. Like Caleb and Joshua, we keep our eyes on the source of our faith and keep on moving forward. Let us, therefore, persevere with excellence in the race of life in which our Heavenly Father has placed each of us.

Pressing On Toward Victory

Timothy DeClue

"Not that I have already reached [the goal] or am already fully mature, but I make every effort to take hold of it because I also have been taken hold of by Christ Jesus. Brothers, I do not consider myself to have taken hold of it. But one thing I do: forgetting what is behind and reaching forward to what is ahead, I pursue as my goal the prize promised by God's heavenly call in Christ Jesus"
(Phil. 3: 12–14 NIV).

Is competition a Christian endeavor? Observing the obnoxious and sometimes violent behavior of a fan at a closely contested sporting event could easily cause us to wonder. Yet, it is almost an unquestioned characteristic of the human experience to compete. We often plunge into competitive actions without even recognizing what it is we are doing. Male suitors compete for the affection of the opposite sex. Businesses compete for market share. Students compete for the best grade on a test, and of course athletes compete for the right to be called champion. Clearly, there is something in each of us which recognizes the competitive environment and responds to it in one way or another. But does God use competition for divine purposes, and is it of significance in His Holy Truth? Is competition biblical?

In The Beginning: "So God created man in His own image; He created him in the image of God; He created them male and female. God blessed them, and God said to them, "Be fruitful, multiply, fill the earth, and subdue it. Rule the fish of the sea, the birds of the sky, and every creature that crawls on the earth" (Gen. 1:27–28 NIV). These are the first divine words heard by human ears. Note what God has chosen to say to his new creation: "Subdue" the earth. There is no subterfuge here. The act of subduing can be argued to be by nature competitive. God is making reference to a fundamental competition he expects humans to win. In this passage we do not see a God whose advice is to lay back and take it easy, but rather to go out and win a battle. Is this first sacred instruction referencing competition a coincidence? Are God's words merely a meeting of chance and moment? I think not. Instead, I believe God is preparing his human creation for the world as he means it to be and as we know it, a battlefield between right and wrong, truth and lies, good and evil.

In Our Minds: "Again I saw under the sun that the race is not to the swift, or the battle to the strong, or bread to the wise, or riches to the discerning, or favor to the skillful; rather, time and chance happen to all of them" (Eccl. 9:11 NIV). As a boy, I remember the special event it was when the Olympics were being held. In the evenings my father and I would sit and watch the various Olympic sports paying particular attention to the American athletes. One marathon runner from an African country stands out clearly in my mind, however. Apparently the runner had been given some shoes that did not fit his feet and had decided it would be better to run barefooted than to run with the ill-fitting shoes. By the time he reached the end of the race, his feet were bloody and he was weaving in such a way that the announcers did not think he would finish. In my memory, I remember asking myself how this runner could have continued to run for so long, even after missing any chance to win. It just didn't make sense; his body was beaten and all thought of victory was gone. As an adult though, I think I understand his actions. The race I watched as a child was not the race he was running. His race was taking place in his mind—a place far from the eyes of the spectators. Finishing the race under such adverse conditions was enough for him to claim victory. There was no need to finish first.

In the same way, I believe God calls us to compete with our minds, and our victory, like that of the marathon runner, is to be defined by the good finish. The inspired words of Ecclesiastes points out that we will not always finish first. Should we then quit? Absolutely not!

In Our Lives: "So I discover this principle: when I want to do good, evil is with me. For in my inner self I joyfully agree with God's law. But I see a different law in the parts of my body, waging war against the law of my mind and taking me prisoner to the law of sin in the parts of my body" (Rom. 7:21–23 NIV). This warfare Paul refers to is unambiguously competitive, and Paul admits to losing from time to time.

Still, Paul does not hint that he would ever consider giving up or losing this war. The competition is fierce, but he does not give in. Instead he says, "Not that I have already reached [the goal] or am already fully mature, but I make every effort to take hold of it because I also have been taken hold of by Christ Jesus. Brothers, I do not consider myself to have taken hold of it. But one thing I do: forgetting what is behind and reaching forward to what is ahead, I pursue as my goal the prize promised by God's heavenly call in Christ Jesus. Therefore, all who are mature should think this way. And if you think differently about anything, God will reveal this to you also" (Phil. 3:12–15 NIV). Paul provides us the perfect example of the competition we fear acknowledging the most: the competition between the sinful nature of our body and the divine orientation of our soul.

In Our Hearts: When the perishable has been clothed with the imperishable, and the mortal with immortality, then the saying that is written will come true: "Now when this corruptible is clothed with incorruptibility, and this mortal is clothed with immortality, then the saying that is written will take place: Death has been swallowed up in victory. O Death, where is your victory? O Death, where is your sting? Now the sting of death is sin, and the power of sin is the law" (1 Cor. 15:54–56 NIV).

It is clear that God includes competition in his view of the world, and that competition is a part of all His creation, including his human creation. But competition is not eternal. Just as in every game played in every sport, eventually the competition ends. The finality of God's competition will be signaled not by a horn or whistle but by the return of Jesus Christ as the victor and the resurrection of the saved to an eternity of glory with him.

9

Putting It into Practice

The Necessity of a Biblical Christian Worldview

Gordon Dutile

Peter instructs us: "But in your hearts set apart Christ as Lord. Always be prepared to give an answer to everyone who asks you to give the reason for the hope that you have. But do this with gentleness and respect" (1 Pet. 3:15 NIV). The word translated *answer* by the NIV literally means "a verbal defense." It is the Greek word from which we get our words apology and apologist. How are we believers going to be able to verbally defend our faith if we do not know what we believe and why we believe it? It is not enough to say that we are Christians. We must demonstrate by word and deed that our faith in Christ drives everything we do.

The more I observe our culture and its spiritual climate, the more I am convicted that the Christian community must equip its members with a solid and sound biblical worldview. What do we mean when we speak of a worldview? It is the framework of life into which everything fits. It is the filter through which every thought, philosophy, and action must pass. Robert A. Harris says,

> One way to understand the idea of a worldview is to say that it's a personal theory of everything. In other words, a worldview is a comprehensive and unifying way of looking at all of life, a means of bringing coherent meaning to one's experiences, thoughts, feelings and so on. Worldviews must

be personally chosen and worked out, and they grow and develop as we learn and gain more knowledge and experience. A worldview includes values, beliefs, commitments, and, attitudes, together with biases and prejudices.[1]

Far too many Christians, whether knowingly or unknowingly, have adopted a two-sphere approach to life. Things that have to do with their relationship with God through Christ fall into the arena of faith; but the things that have to do with the physical, everyday world fall into the arena of that which can be proven by experimentation and empirical data. They act as if the two spheres should not interact, and that to allow them to do so results in some kind of false union, an unholy alliance. That is why some can claim to be Christian and yet function in a worldly setting as though Christ had nothing to do with their actions. From the biblical perspective, not to integrate them is a false dichotomy that leaves the Lord out of a portion of life. The statement, "Jesus is either Lord of all or not Lord at all," comes to mind. A truly biblical Christian worldview sees the totality of life through the lens of a personal relationship with Jesus the Christ.

This worldview integrates three fundamental issues: (1) Creation—How did I get here? (2) The fall—Why am I like I am? (3) Redemption—What can be done about my condition?[2] Every Christian must come to the settled conviction that "In the beginning God created the heavens and the earth" (Gen. 1:1 NIV). The writer of Hebrews states, "By faith we understand that the worlds were prepared by the word of God, so that what is seen was not made out of things which are visible" (Heb. 11:3 NASB). A lot of discussion may occur about how God did it and what kind of time frame it involved. But for the Christian, there can be no question as to who did it.

People from various persuasions have offered theories and explanations about why wrong exists in the human arena. The Bible makes

1. Robert A. Harris, *The Integration of Faith and Learning: A Worldview Approach* (Eugene, OR: Cascade Books, 2004), p. 77.

2. For an in-depth discussion of these, see Nancy Pearcey, *Total Truth: Liberating Christianity from Its Cultural Captivity* (Wheaton, IL: Crossway Books, 2004), pp. 82–95. Also, Cornelius Plantinga Jr., *Engaging God's World: A Christian Vision of Faith, Learning, and Living* (Grand Rapids, MI: Wm. B. Eerdmans, 2002), pp. 17–100.

it clear. The first humans chose to do it their way instead of God's; they said *my* will, not *your* will. That choice determined that all of humanity as offspring of the first Adam would be sinners. The universality of sin is proclaimed in both the Old and New Testaments. "When they sin against you—for there is no one who does not sin—" (1 Kings 8:46a NIV). "Everyone has turned away, they have together become corrupt; there is no one who does good, not even one" (Ps. 130:3 NIV). "For all have sinned and fall short of the glory of God" (Rom. 3:23 NIV). "But the Scripture declares that the whole world is a prisoner of sin . . ." (Gal. 3:22a NIV). As a result of this rebellion, humanity does not seek God. Instead we hide from God, as Adam and Eve did. The psalmist says, "The Lord has looked down from heaven upon the sons of men, to see if there are any who understand, who seek after God. They have all turned aside; together they have become corrupt; there is no one who does good, not even one" (Ps. 14:2–3 NASB).

Left to himself, a human is in an inescapable predicament. Paul's description of this difficult plight says, "And you were dead in your trespasses and sins, in which you formerly walked according to the course of this world, according to the prince of the power of the air, of the spirit that is now working in the sons of disobedience. Among them we too all formerly lived in the lusts of our flesh, indulging the desires of the flesh and of the mind, and were by nature children of wrath, even as the rest" (Eph. 2:1–3 NASB).

Paul makes it clear that left alone a person is hopelessly doomed. We can be grateful that the story does not end there. The apostle continues, "*But God* (emphasis mine), being rich in mercy, because of His great love with which He loved us, even when we were dead in our transgressions, made us alive together with Christ (by grace you have been saved), and raised us up with Him, and seated us with Him in the heavenly *places*, in Christ Jesus, in order that in the ages to come He might show the surpassing riches of His grace in kindness toward us in Christ Jesus" (Eph. 2:4–7 NASB).

Every other worldview has man achieving his deliverance by his own effort. Christianity reveals that redemption is accomplished by the intervention of God. Notice in the passages from Ephesians that when the human is the subject of the action, there is spiritual death and damnation. When God is the subject of the action, there is life and deliverance. In the Garden of Eden, the first Adam said no to God's will and yes to self and plunged his offspring into sin. Throughout Jesus' life on earth and in the Garden of Gethsemane, the second Adam said yes to God's will and no to self and provided humanity an escape from condemnation.

It is through this three-pronged filter that the Christian must view life. The believer must not compartmentalize life, or segment it. Everything he or she does is to be done to honor God. "So whether you eat or drink or whatever you do, do it all for the glory of God" (1 Cor. 10:31 NIV). It is imperative that Christians develop a strong biblical worldview that impacts the entirety of life, including their academic, professional, recreational, and personal lives. Dr. David Dockery, in the introduction to *Shaping a Christian Worldview*, says,

> Christian worldview is not just one's personal faith expression, not just a theory. It is an all-consuming way of life, applicable to all spheres of life. . . . A Christian worldview is not built on two types of truth (religious and philosophical or scientific) but on a universal principle and all-embracing system that shapes religion, natural and social sciences, law, history, health care, the arts, the humanities, and all disciplines of study with application for all of life.[3]

Each Christian is to live life in a way that the Lordship of Christ is evident. The lost world needs to recognize that believers have a hope that is beyond this world and age. Then they will inquire as to the reason for that hope. It is essential that at that moment the Christian be able to give a verbal defense with gentleness and respect. May we live by Paul's admonition: "For though we live in the world, we do not wage war as the world does. The weapons we fight with are not the weapons of the world. On the contrary, they have divine power to demolish arguments and every pretension that sets itself up against the knowledge of God, and we take captive every thought to make it obedient to Christ" (2 Cor. 10:3–5 NIV).

3. David S. Dockery and Gregory Alan Thornbury, ed., *Shaping a Christian Worldview: The Foundations of Christian Higher Education* (Nashville, TN: Broadman and Holman, 2002), p. 2.

A Challenge

David Wesley Whitlock

OF COURSE, writers hope not just to be read, but to be heard. The hope of each contributor to this work is that you have been challenged to think (or rethink) each of the topics addressed. Our hope is that you have come to the conclusion that as a Christian, God has placed (or will place) you in a unique position of influence. Others will watch you. They will observe whether or not your Christianity makes any difference in the way you conduct yourself professionally and personally. People are hungry to see consistency in the lives of believers. This is especially true, I am convinced, in the marketplace.

If you are a Christian, will you prayerfully consider the words penned in this small book of devotions? Will you commit to a life that is marked by integrity, service, respect, charity, faithfulness, truthfulness, humility and perseverance? Will you consider whether or not your own faith is so private and hidden that it has no impact or relevance to your life as a professional? Remember the words found in James: "Foolish man! Are you willing to learn that faith without works is useless?" (James 2:20 NKJV). Prayerfully consider how your worldview impacts the way you conduct yourself at work, at home, in private, and when no one is watching. Remember the concept of your stewardship of experience. God desires to use everything you have experienced including your education and your work life.

For those who have yet to believe and place their faith in the person of Jesus Christ, there is this challenge. Examine your own life in light of a biblical worldview. Each of the contributors to this book has achieved personal and professional success and enjoyed many years of education and advanced degrees. Yet, at our core, each of us faces the same problem. We know deep down that there is a God and that we are separated from him. Our challenge to you is to read the following brief explanation of being right with God. Our prayer is that you would open your mind to how God may speak to you.

Our Problem: God created us in his own image to have an abundant life. The first man and woman, Adam and Eve, were made perfect and lived without sin until they rebelled against God. Now, all of Adam's descendants, including you, live under the curse of death and sin. Everyone has deliberately chosen to disobey God. In our sinful state, none of us is able to seek after God. The result is our separation from God and the sentence of death and hell upon us.

As it is written, *"There is none who understands; there is none who seeks after God. They have all gone out of the way; they have together become unprofitable; There is none who does good, no not one"* (Rom. 3:10–12 NKJV). *"Now we know that whatever the law says, it says to those who are under the law, that every mouth may be stopped, and all the world may become guilty before God. Therefore by the deeds of the law no flesh will be justified in His sight, for by the law is the knowledge of sin"* (Rom. 3:19–20 NKJV). *"For all have sinned and fall short of the glory of God"* (Rom. 3:23 NKJV). *"For the wages of sin is death, but the gift of God is eternal life in Christ Jesus our Lord"* (Rom. 6:23 NKJV). Our situation is desperate. We are separated from God and incapable of doing anything about it. We have sinned and are under the curse of death and punishment.

God's Answer: Though we are deserving of punishment and judgment, God is merciful and loving. God provided an answer to our problem: Jesus the Christ, meaning the Messiah or Savior. Jesus lived a perfect life without any sin. He offered himself as the sacrifice for our sin. Jesus took the punishment of death upon himself. He died on the cross and three days later rose from the dead, securing forgiveness and eternal life for all who surrender to him and trust in him alone. He paid the penalty for our sin. Discover the greatest joy known to man—knowing the God who created you. Are you humbled and grieved to learn of your sin? Do you want to be forgiven and made right with God?

"The Lord is merciful and gracious, slow to anger and plenteous in mercy" (Ps. 103:8 NKJV). *"For God so loved the world that He gave His only begotten Son, that whoever believes in Him should not perish but have everlasting life"* (John 3:16 NKJV). *"But God demonstrates His own love for us in this: While we were still sinners, Christ died for us"* (Rom. 5:8 NKJV). *"And as it is appointed unto man once to die, and after this the judgment, so Christ was once offered to bear the sins of many; and unto them that look for him shall he appear the second time without sin unto salvation"* (Heb. 9:27 NKJV). Are you humbled and grieved to learn of your sin? Do you want to be forgiven and made right with God?

Our Response: We must confess and repent (turn away from our sins) and surrender our lives totally to him. God commands you to repent and believe in the Lord Jesus. God even grants you the faith required to believe. True converts will have enduring evidence of their salvation and will love and fellowship with God's people in a local church. They will bear spiritual fruit, and they will endure unto the end as they watch and eagerly wait for the Lord to return as he promised.

"If you confess with your mouth the Lord Jesus and believe in your heart that God has raised Him from the dead, you will be saved. For whoever calls upon the name of the Lord will be saved" (Rom. 10:9, 13 NKJV). *"For it is by grace you have been saved, through faith and this is not of yourselves, it is the gift of God not by works, so that no one can boast"* (Eph. 2.8–9 NKJV). *"And let us consider one another in order to stir up love and good works, not forsaking the assembling of ourselves together, as is the manner of some, but exhorting one another, and so much the more as you see the Day approaching"* (Heb. 10:24–25 NKJV). *"But the fruit of the Spirit is love, joy, peace, longsuffering, kindness, goodness, faithfulness, gentleness, self-control"* (Gal. 5:22–23 NKJV). *"In My Father's house are many mansions; if it were not so, I would have told you. I go to prepare a place for you. And if I go and prepare a place for you, I will come again and receive you to Myself; that where I am, there you may be also. And where I go you know, and the way you know"* (John 14:2–4 NKJV).

Pray to God and confess your sins to him. Turn from your sin and ask him to forgive you. Place your faith in Jesus, his death on a cross in your place, and his resurrection from the dead. Surrender your will to

Jesus and find a local church to help you in your Christian walk. Then, as Eph. 4:1 urges, walk worthy of your calling. In doing so, may you find yourself living and working as a *Psalm 15 professional.*

DWW